COFFEE AND PRAYERS
Morning Devotionals

By Billy Ray Philley Jr.

Text Copyright ®2021 Billy Ray Philley Jr.

Copyright ©2021 Coffee and Prayers

Publishing Copyright ©2021 Laurel Rose Publishing

Laurel Rose Publishing
www.laurelrosepublishing.com
laurelrosepublishing@gmail.com

ISBN-13: 978-1-944583-33-0

This book are the thoughts and opinions of the author.
No part of this book may be reproduced, stored in a retrieval system, or transmitted by any

Coffee and Prayers

Acknowledgement

Chad Martin with Laurel Rose publishing
Abe Draper photographing
Ryan Matthews

Special thanks to my family and friends for the support and encouragement.

About the Author

Billy started writing morning devotionals in 2012. Before long, he added short stories about life with scripture references and titled it "Coffee and Prayers".
As a gifted writer, he captured an audience of Facebook followers.

He was encouraged to write a book. His work was not complete as he went to be with the Lord before he could finish it.

In his honor, his hard work was finally published
I hope you enjoy reading this book as I was blessed to forward it.

As he always said "If this post helps just one person, it was worth writing it."

Publisher's Note

We made a decision early on in the process of putting this book together to reflect Billy's actual posts. We didn't take liberties with his wording nor with some of the grammar because we feel it would have lost the character and meaning of his impactful writing. We hope you enjoy, appreciate and are moved by Billy's morning devotionals.

Coffee and Prayers

Coffee and Prayers this Freezing Cold Friday Morning.

It's been a long week, but the weekend is about here. I've posted this before, but I think maybe something light hearted may be what some may need to hear today.

I was thinking this morning about a story that a lot of people around me know. Years ago, when I was a teenager, I asked my Grandmother (Gladys Hood Philley) whom we called "Nenny",

"Why did you name Dad Billy, knowing that it would rhyme with his last name?" (I of course am a Jr.) She replied "That was my nephew Bonnie Hood's idea to name your daddy Billy. He thought it would be a good name. So me and your Paw Paw named him Billy Philley."

I asked "You have a NEPHEW named Bonnie?" Well apparently so and it wasn't an uncommon name for a man back in the day. So I then knew how my dad and then my name came to be. Of course all of my life people have had a laugh over my name. I've even had people ask "Did you know your name rhymes?"

Really? Why no, I hadn't noticed! Thank you for pointing that out to me!

Coffee and Prayers

Fast forward several years later. I can't remember how old I was but I must've been in my early 20's. I was at Parker Cemetery at Alva, Mississippi, way back in Webster County

at the graves of my Grandmother and Grandfather. To get to this cemetery, you literally have to drive through a pasture. If you are there, you are there on purpose. I was standing there at my Grandparent's graves. And elderly gentleman drove up. He casually walked down the hill to the grave side where I was. He walked up to me and said "You're here at Uncle Howard and Aunt Glady's grave, you must be kin to me." He then stuck his hand out and said "I'm Bonnie Hood." I shook his hand and said "I'm Billy Philley, and I'm going to kill you!" I told him about what Nenny had told me, and he and I had a good laugh about it.

It was sort of a "Boy named Sue" moment. We stood there and talked family for what must have been a couple of hours.

My point with this? Nothing heavy or "profound". Just that I think that it is important to have a good sense of humor. To be able to laugh at yourself, to laugh at life sometimes.
Many people don't realize that Jesus taught with humor. When He spoke of removing the plank from your own eye? That was hilarious to the culture of

that day! A camel going through the eye of a needle? He had the Jews of that day laughing so hard! The blind leading the blind and falling in a ditch? This was "rolling on the floor" laughter material. Some just don't see it. If we lived 2,000 years ago we would better get that.

Think of the personality Jesus had to simply walk up to a group of fishermen and saying "Follow Me, and I will make you a fisher of men." They left their jobs immediately and followed Him! They weren't hypnotized! They were captured by His dynamic personality. He had a tremendous personality. He knew when to use humor and when not to.

I think we simply do not these days laugh at ourselves enough. We don't laugh at LIFE enough. Some things just aren't funny. True enough. Our comedies can turn tragic in the blink of an eye. The thing is, we need to laugh. We need light moments. We need balance in our lives. We need humor to balance out the drama that tends to plague us at times. Don't be AFRAID to laugh. Don't be afraid to laugh at life. God created humor! I picture Jesus as smiling. I picture Him as laughing. I picture His countenance as joyful.

Take time daily to see the humor in all of life. If we let even life's annoyances become humorous to us, then we don't let it ruin our day.

Coffee and Prayers

Have a great day and LAUGH!
"A merry heart does good, like medicine,
But a broken spirit dries the bones." Proverbs 17:22

Coffee and prayers this Saturday morning.

Yesterday I was looking at a movie display in a store. As I was searching for a certain movie, I saw the movie "Contagion" on display. It's a pretty good movie that starts with Gweneth Paltrow on a business trip to Southeast Asia (Thailand I believe) She was an executive for a large corporation that had just closed a deal there. The caption on the screen said "Day 2". She wanted to meet the chef of this Asian restaurant there and thank him for the excellent meal, which featured a whole roasted small pig. She shook his hand and they had several pictures made together. On her return trip home, she had a layover in another city and called an old boyfriend who lived there. She was not feeling well by this time, and when she got home to her husband and son the next day, she was very sick. Within hours, her 6 year old son was sick. By the next day, she fell out, was hospitalized and died within hours. Her son had died within hours as well. Her husband never got sick. He was immune to this disease.

By now, people all over, hundreds of them were displaying these same symptoms and dying within a few days. In fact, from Southeast Asia this same disease was spreading. Thousands dying was becoming tens of thousands, then hundreds of thousands, and growing.

As the story expanded, the doctors from the CDC were discussing how this unknown illness was spreading. One doctor (Kate Winslet) said that humans touch their faces thousands of times each day, after touching thousands of surfaces that thousands of people have touched.

The disease was highly contagious. Spread by mere incidental contact. Some were immune to the disease, and after exposure showed no symptoms.

As the disease spread and thousands of people were dying, it caused a breakdown of basic services.

There was rioting, looting, and as food was disributed, people were being robbed for their rations. Worldwide panic, fear, and mistrust of everyone else got worse and worse.

Coffee and Prayers

A vaccine was developed, but it was done by a "draft" type basis. Dates were drawn at random and those whose birthday was on that day could get their vaccine that day.

During the investigation, scientists discovered that it was some type of unknown disease, a mix of pig and bat somehow was at the root of it. Some had a natural immunity, but most of the population did not. Merely touching something that an infected person has touched will infect a person.

At the end of the movie, a "flashback" scene and a caption that read "Day 1" showed a group of bats in the jungle, feeding on bananas. These bats were then seen hanging from the rafters of a barn, and a piece of banana dropped from the mouth of a bat, onto the floor of the barn where a pig ate it. Later, the pig was gathered up along with a

few other small pigs. Then, an Asian chef was shown stuffing apple slices into one of the pig's mouth. He was told that an American woman wanted to meet him and thank him for the meal. He wipes his hand on his apron and then goes out and shakes the hand of this American woman (Paltrow).

This is how a worldwide pandemic began. One person didn't wash his hands.

Coffee and Prayers

It reminded me of gossip. That's how gossip spreads. One careless person. It spreads to others by casual contact. Some are immune, most are not. Some will hear, and "wash their hands", so to speak, and therefore not spread it.

It will "kill" some. Kill their reputation, kill their respect from others. Far too many base their opinion of some by what someone else "gossips" about them. Gossip is a contagion. It's a disease that spreads like wildfire. It's a killer of reputation; it's a killer of friendships, relationships, and careers. I have been in classes in both civilian and military life where an instructor has whispered something to one person, told that person to whisper it to the next, and soon. The instructor would then ask the last person what was said. It would always, without fail, be nothing close to what the first person was told.

Gossip grows with each person it goes to. It gets worse for the person gossiped about.

The Bible says much about gossip and gossips. 1 Timothy and Proverbs come to mind.

Have YOU ever been gossiped about? Has anyone ever told you something about yourself that you had absolutely no clue about and was 100% false?

Coffee and Prayers

If not, you're either on an island alone, or a hermit likely.

We are all guilty in the spread of it at times, aren't we?

Just like a disease, we must either be immune to gossip, or when we hear it, wash our hands of it immediately, lest we spread it.

Gossip. A contagion. A disease. A killer.

Let's not spread gossip. If we didn't hear that certain thing from that certain person with our own ears, see it with our own eyes, and we spread it with our own mouth, then we are spreading a lie, 100% of the time. Have a great day everyone.

"Where there is no wood, the fire goes out; and where there is no talebearer, strife ceases. As charcoal is to burning coals, and wood to fire, so is a contentious man to kindle strife." Proverbs 26:20-21

Coffee and Prayers

Coffee and prayers this freezing cold morning.

We can at least see the weekend from here.

I was thinking about a Miranda Lambert song that has been out a while now. "This Ain't My Mamas Broken Heart." It's about a girl who goes kinda crazy after a break-up, but her mother is much too proper and admonishes her for it. One is NOT to show any public displays of emotion.

Here are a few verses of the song:

"Powder your nose, paint your toes
Line your lips and keep'em closed,
Cross your legs, dot your eyes
And never let 'em see you cry.
Go and fix your make up, well it's just a break up
Run and hide your crazy and start actin' like a lady
'Cause I raised you better, gotta keep it together
Even when you fall apart
But this ain't my mama's broken heart."

That's the same way some are. Keep it all hidden, keep it quiet. Never confess a sin; never admit a weakness .Never show that you have an addiction. After all, the "show" is important isn't it?

Coffee and Prayers

I've broken every commandment of God. I've done everything and anything under the sun. I'm a sinner. I have weaknesses. I have vulnerabilities. Don't we all?

Yesterday a friend of mine and I were talking. He said that he had had some stop coming to his small group when they would hear of others admit their sins and shortcomings.

The small groups I have been in have been some of the best spiritual experiences I've had. The way believers bond, the way believers can take that "mask" off. The way that believers know that they have a safe place to discuss their concerns, their problems, and so on.

There is confidentiality, and there is accountability. Most of all, there is love and there is prayer.
I once had someone say that small groups sound like "pity parties", where everyone sits around and complains and whines. I won't go into my response, but I will just say that you can't expect lost people to act like saved people.

Some don't want to talk about it. After all, they don't even discuss it with GOD; they sure aren't going to talk about it to others.

Coffee and Prayers

They are, however, quick to point out others sins. There are some who even love it when anyone who is a Christian falls, makes a public mistake, commits some sin that becomes public. They love to tear "that so -called Christian "down to the ground. They HATE it when a Christian admits that they also sin at times. It takes away their "GOTCHA!" moments.

David was a man after God's own heart. And David committed adultery and then murder to cover it up. It was no surprise to God. It is God whom put in place forgiveness. Forgiveness for all of us.

Do you know the story of the man who used to persecute and even kill Christians? He hated them. You may have heard the name of Paul. He, after his conversion, wrote about two thirds of our New Testament.

From Genesis to Revelation, from Adam to Paul, all in the Bible were sinners except Jesus.

And look at that! God lays it all out, right there for us all to see!

Here is some news. "Those so called Christians" ARE going to sin. They are going to fall in a ditch. They may cover it up, they may hide it, and they may deny it. They, as all of us are, sinners saved by grace. And their sin of covering their sin is no worse than those of us who sin and admit it. Sin is sin. God doesn't grade sin on a sliding scale of "Not that bad" to "hell deserving terrible." All sin is sin, and it's all equal. The good news is that Christ paid for it ALL on the cross. He died for ALL sin. Past, present and future.

We should not (though we all do, to a point) keep tabs on other's sins. Let's all remember that when we are His, we are HIS. And we ought not be discussing what others did and how "terrible" it was, when we are just as bad.

Have a great day everyone.

"For there is not a just man on earth who does good And does not sin.
Also do not take to heart everything people say, Lest you hear your servant cursing you.
For many times, also, your own heart has known That even you have cursed others. " Ecclesiastes 7:20-22

Coffee and Prayers

Coffee and Prayers this Cool, Foggy Monday Morning.

I posted this back in October but God placed it on my heart to post it again. Someone perhaps will be helped by it I pray.

I was thinking about a story that I heard several years ago.

"Mary" was a very bitter woman. Her husband had been murdered in cold blood when his little store had been robbed one night. She had struggled for 7 years since his death, raising 2 kids.
She had even dropped out of church. She hadn't always been bitter, but the death of her husband and the years of struggle had caused her heart to turn that way. Hatred for her husband's killer had torso it changed her.

During the trial of the murderer, she remembered the look on Marcus' face. He was a huge black man with a V-shaped scar above his left eye. He had a look of hatred. He showed no remorse at his trial. He had even given the jury the "finger."

So seven years after the trial, through a series of events and a friend of a friend, she got word that Marcus had got saved through a prison ministry.

Coffee and Prayers

Marcus had become a "model prisoner" since his salvation. He had gained the warden's attention, this man who was serving life without parole. His behavior had turned 180 degrees.
Mary was even angrier now.

She wanted to visit Marcus in prison and tell him exactly what she thought of him and the hell that he had put her and her family through.

She made arrangements to see Marcus. As he entered the room and sat down across the table from her, she saw something in his countenance. He looked totally different. The menacing scar even now didn't look so scary.

He looked at her and told her that the night he robbed and killed her husband, that her husband had actually prayed for him, rather than himself. He said "Ma'am, his last words were 'Dear Lord, please forgive this man.' His words haunted me for five years. Then I started reading the Bible, I prayed, and I asked Jesus into my life. Ma'am, Jesus saved me. I will spend my life here in jail, but I'd rather be here and saved than free and lost. Your husband's prayer saved me."

She saw tears streaming down his huge face. She realized that was exactly something that her husband would have done. She had spent years imaging her husband's last minute in terror. Instead, he was in prayer for his killer!

Now Mary felt those years of anger and bitterness melt away. She told Marcus that she also now forgave him, although she hadn't until then. Marcus said "Ma'am, now you is free. You been in prison all this time. Now you free." They prayed together. After she left, she and Marcus wrote back and forth for nearly a year.

Then one day the warden called her. He wanted her to know that Marcus had been stabbed and killed as he tried to break up a fight. He had saved another inmate's life as he lost his own.
Mary hung up the phone and imagined the reunion in heaven as her husband greeted Marcus there.

Isn't that what forgiveness does? It releases us from our prison.

Forgiveness. It's what our entire faith is based upon. Forgiveness. As our Savior hung on the cross He asked for the forgiveness of those who crucified Him. Forgiveness.

Without it what are we? Who are we? Mary was indeed in prison those years she hated Marcus. Forgiveness set her free. Are you free today?

Coffee and Prayers

Who have you not forgiven? If you've not forgiven yourself, start there. Forgiveness. Such a beautiful word that must be more than a word, it must come with turning that key in your heart and setting the captive free.

Have a great day everyone.

"'For if you forgive men their trespasses, your heavenly Father will also forgive you. But if you do not forgive men their trespasses, neither will your Father forgive your trespasses.'" Matthew 6:14-15

Coffee and prayers this Thursday morning.

Four hours of sleep to get me through this day means a very long day.

Before I post, I wanted to say that God reminded me of something this morning. Because He indeed spoke the world into existence, literally BREATHED the air we

breathe, with every breath, we are breathing HIS breath. His breath is in our lungs.

A young man was in his senior year of high school. He had been promised a car for graduation. He and

Coffee and Prayers

his father shopped around, found the one he wanted from a picture in a magazine , and that's the one they had decided upon. The entire second semester of his senior year he longed for that car and couldn't wait to drive it to college. Graduation day came, and he got his diploma. When they arrived home, he was a little surprised to not see the car in the driveway.

His father told him that he couldn't wait to give him his gift.

His father handed him a box, the young man opened it, expecting the keys to his car. Instead, it was a Bible. The young man threw the Bible to the floor and stormed out. He left home and never returned. He never spoke to his father again. Twenty or so years passed before he got the word that his father had passed away. He returned to settle his father's estate and sell everything. He was still bitter and angry after all those years. He entered the house and went to his old room and found it just as he'd left it all those years ago , except on his bed laid that Bible that his father gave him graduation day . The one he'd thrown down in anger. He snatched it up; anxious for it to be the first thing he'd get rid of. As he did, an envelope fell out with his name on it. He opened it and inside was a hand written card from his father, a picture of the car from the magazine, and a cashier's check for the amount of the car, dated his graduation day. The card said "Congratulations son. I am looking forward to going and getting this with you. I love you, Dad."

The young man had needlessly been angry all those years. He threw the word of God back at his father because he thought he deserved more. He expected more. He wasted

his life, and broke his father's heart, when all along God's word had a treasure for him.

There are so many people these days that, sadly, much like this young man, reject God's word when they think it has no meaning for them, nothing to offer them. A disappointment. God's word is so rejected outright by so many because they think it has nothing for them but "dos and don'ts".

The Bible has been maligned, slandered, rejected, burned, banned, doubted, dismissed, and threatened. It has been predicted to be extinct for thousands of years. Jesus, however, said in Mark 13:31 "Heaven and earth will pass away, but My words will by no means pass away."

It's the best-selling book of all time. The average Christian family, I once read, owns at least 4 Bibles. If all Bibles were only read and followed, believed and all within practiced, think of how much better our lives, our families, our nation and this world would be.

The best analogy I've heard about the Bible is that it's God's love letter to us. It's His "logos", the written word for us, and when we seek all He has for us, it becomes the "rhema", the living word, God's word. It holds so much hidden treasure for us. But when we throw it down because it's not what we think it should be, we never find it. When we don't seek God's face in prayer, when we don't seek answers in His word, then we miss His love letter and His treasure for us.

His word is vital to us.

The times that I was all alone, those times I was so far from home, I could touch His word, as I kept it by me at all times. It was and still is my comfort, my light, my path, my compass, my instructions, my guardrail.

Have you read His love letter to you? Have you sought that treasure within it? It is so much better than a new car. Itis a new life, an eternal life with Him, once we are His. Have a great day everyone.

"For the word of God is living and powerful, and sharper than any two-edged sword, piercing even to the division of soul and spirit, and of joints and marrow, and is a discerner of the thoughts and intents of the heart. And there is no creature hidden from His sight, but all things are naked and open to the eyes of Him to whom we must give account." Hebrews 4:12-13

Coffee and prayers this freezing cold morning.

Much to do today.

As I drive, I listen to a country station that plays older country songs. One that I heard the other day that I had almost forgotten about was "Coat of Many Colors" by

Dolly Parton. It's a song written by Dolly that is the true story of when she was a child and someone had given her family a box of rags. Her family was very poor, and she didn't have a coat. Her mother sewed the rags together and made her a coat. In the song, she says that her mother told the story of Joseph's coat of many colors from the Bible.

She was so proud of her colorful coat that her mother had made for her, but when she wore it to school, the other kids were laughing and making fun of her coat. She told the other kids that her

Coffee and Prayers

mother made it with love, and it was worth more than all their clothes.

In fact, that very coat is on display at Dollywood. She's kept it all these years.

So what do we consider as valuable? What do we consider priceless? Does it have to come with an expensive price tag? Yes expensive gifts are nice, but what about gifts that are from the heart?

What small gifts do you have that you treasure the most?

I know I have things that are not pricey, but were from the heart, and therefore priceless.
I wear a watch that Cindy gave me. It's not a Rolex, it didn't come from a jewelry store, but I've worn it every day for 3 years. It's valuable to me because it was from her heart. It being on my wrist is almost like she's holding my hand.

I have a little ceramic duck that my daughter Nikki gave me when she was about 6 years
old. It likely didn't cost a dollar, but is priceless to me. She may not even remember giving it. I have 2 quilts that my grandma made for me that I consider to be priceless. I have other things that my parents, kids, etc. have given me that are priceless to me,

even though the world may not consider them to be worth a dime.

I have boxes still from some things that I have received over the years. Even the box means a lot to me. A gift isn't valuable just because it cost a lot. The heart behind it is the main thing to me. What are your treasures? What do you consider to be most valuable? Is it only that which cost the most? Or is it that which was from the heart?

Our greatest gift is the gift of salvation. Our salvation cost us nothing, yet Jesus gave all that He had for it. He paid the ultimate price for it. Are you grateful for it daily?

What is most valuable in life to you? Is that where your heart is? Is your heart where your treasure is?

We have a gift that the world may not consider worth a dime, yet it was worth the life of the Son of God. It just can't get any more valuable than that.

Have a great day everyone.

"'Do not lay up for yourselves treasures on earth, where moth and rust destroy and where thieves break in and steal; but lay up for yourselves treasures in heaven, where neither moth nor rust destroys and where thieves do not break in and steal. For where your treasure is, there your heart will be also.'" Matthew 6:19-21

Coffee and Prayers this Lord's Day.

As I was driving and listening to a country oldies station one day a few years ago, I heard an old Waylon song, "Ladies Love Outlaws." It's a song describing how 3 "good girls" went after "bad boys."

It got me to thinking about just how true that is in so many cases. So many times growing up, through the teen "dating years "I heard that girls don't want a "good guy", they want the "bad boys."

It was also true of guys and "bad girls" so many times. Guys didn't want the sweet, pretty, good hearted "girl next-door." They wanted to date the bad girls. They didn't want one that they could take home to mom, they wanted the bad ones.

I suppose in many ways it's always been that way, but it seems as if the attraction to "bad" is stronger than ever.

Coffee and Prayers

I never watched it, but for several seasons, a very popular TV show was a show called "Breaking Bad", about a man who is a meth manufacturer. There was a TV show "Hannibal" about a serial killer, Hannibal Lecter. There was also a TV show about Norman Bates, based on the movie "Psycho."

ABC had a short lived series about people who have made a deal with the devil called "666 Park Avenue".

Worse than the media embracing evil is what people do. There were thousands of people who went to the funerals of Bonnie Parker and Clyde Barrow (Bonnie and Clyde). What is it about common criminals that would attract law-abiding citizens?

Mass murderers such as Charles Manson and others get fan mail in prison.

I knew of a man several years ago whose wife left him and their small daughter for a man who was just released from Parchman Prison. I know of women whose husbands just up and left for some woman they met online, and there are women who do the same.

Coffee and Prayers

People risk or give up family for the "bad boy" or "bad girl". They'd rather live the "bad life" than a normal, peaceful one.

These stories seldom end well. Remember Samson? He chose the "bad girl", Delilah. He was super strong, could kill thousands, yet his choice for a mate was his downfall. This mighty champion of Israel ended up a blind slave when he chose the "bad girl."

Choosing the bad over the good never works out and never ends well.

The Bible says we reap what we sow. (Gal 6:7).

Woman choses the bad boy, then wonders why she ends up hurt by him. A man choses a bad girl and then ends up being heartbroken by her.

It's like choosing a rattlesnake for a pet. It may take a while, but sooner or later, the snake will bite.

Choosing bad, choosing evil, pursuing it, relishing it. It may be "fun" for a while. Sin usually is "fun". If it wasn't, no one would be doing it.

Hebrews 11:25 says that Moses chose the affliction of his people over the "pleasures of sin for a season."

Coffee and Prayers

There is a fascination with the bad, the evil. But it never ends well. Those who followed Manson ended up dead or in prison. Those who follow the "gangster" lifestyle end up dead or in prison. We know that even one third of the angels followed Satan when he was cast from heaven. People enjoy it, for a while. But the ride ends soon, and then all that is left is someone whose reputation is that of which lifestyle they've lived.

Even still, God is there after it all with mercy and grace.

His grace endures, but there are still the consequences.

We all sin. All of us. Daily. None are perfect. But are we pursuing that which is leading us to more sin? Leading us to more consequences?

We should seek what it is that God sets before us. When we do, we won't have those consequences of pursuing bad.

Have a great day everyone. "Seek good and not evil, That you may live; So the Lord God of hosts will be with you, as

you have spoken. Hate evil, love good; Establish justice in the gate." Amos 5:14-15

Coffee and Prayers

Coffee and Prayers this Tuesday Morning.

With all of this talk recently about women's marching I wanted to give some information about the women in my family who have marched.

Both of my grandmothers marched. They marched into the kitchen each morning at 4 AM. They prepared the family breakfast. They then marched out into the fields where they worked just as hard and right alongside the men. They received wages equal to the men. They chopped cotton all day long for 50 cents a day. That's right 50 cents a day. And I do not mean 8 o'clock until 5 o'clock. I mean daylight until dark.

During harvest season they also made wages equal to the man. They made 25 cents per hundred. That's right. They made 25 cents per hundred pounds of cotton. The exact same thing that the men made. Cotton weighs the same thing regardless if it's picked by a man or a woman.

After a long hard day of work in the fields, they would then march home and prepare the evening meal. They would also take care of the children.

My mother also marched. When she was old enough she marched into the fields and worked

Coffee and Prayers

also. When she got grown she marched into the workforce and sometimes worked two jobs. When she decided that a job did not pay enough for her, she would move on to a better paying job.

She also marched into the kitchen each morning to prepare breakfast for the family. She marched into the laundry room and taught her children how to do laundry just as her mother had done with her. The same with my step mother and my mother in law. My wife also marched. She marched around the house wrangling a house full of daughters while studying to become a nurse. She worked and studied at the same time. She marched from her job to school to better herself. She marched into the kitchen to prepare meals; she marched into the laundry room to make sure the family had clean clothes to wear.

My daughters marched. They marched to get an education. They marched to get a job. They march now taking care of their own families. They march into the kitchen to prepare meals. They march into the laundry room to make sure the family has clean clothes to wear.

Neither my grandmothers, mother, wife nor daughters need any millionaire singer or Hollywood actress to try to teach any of them about "dignity".

Coffee and Prayers

They all have dignity on their own. They don't need some silly ignorant spoiled brats dressing up as women private parts to try to teach them about "dignity". My mother, step-Mother, wife, mother in law and daughters all have more dignity in their little fingers than those people have in their entire bodies.

They did not need to make ridiculous looking costumes. They did not need to fly to Washington. They did not need to march in a parade. They did not need to listen to the rantings of people who sound as if they should be committed to a mental institution. They do not need anyone to tell them that they are "equal".

The women that I know and love, including all of my friends and the rest of my family get their self-worth from the Lord. They do not need someone in Washington to tell them what their "worth" is. They knew, and still know, that God created them to do the things that men cannot do. They know that God made them vastly superior to men in many ways. They also know that there are things that they were designed by God to do, just as there are things God designed men to do.

Please do not say that you are representing "all women".

Coffee and Prayers

The women that I know and love do quite well representing themselves, as do 99.9% of all of my women friends.

And none of you Hollywood millionaires and vulgar "entertainers" can hold a candle to them. They are women who truly ROAR. They don't whine and complain.

And that is all that I have to say about that.

Coffee and Prayers this Friday Morning.

The other day, I watched an episode of Andy Griffith. In this episode, Andy's son Opie and his friend had gone to the carnival that was in town. Opie went to the shooting gallery and did quite well. He decided that he'd try to win electric razors for his dad's upcoming birthday. The carnival hucksters running the shooting gallery of course were running a scam, where they'd let someone use the only "good" gun, then they'd switch up and give them one with bent sights. Opie of course lost his money and was disappointed. He then went and enlisted Goober to help him. They of course ran the same scam on him.

Coffee and Prayers

Goober, visibly upset, went alone to ask Andy to reassure him that he was indeed a good shot. And Goober accidentally revealed to Andy that Opie had been trying to win him the electric razor. Andy told Goober to get Opie, bring him back to the carnival later, and not say anything about him knowing. Andy changed out of his uniform, and he and Hellen Crump went to the shooting gallery "undercover." Andy right away saw the problem and wouldn't let them switch guns on him. And he won Hellen nearly everything in the booth except the razor.

When the hucksters got angry, he showed them his badge, and told him that a little boy was coming back , and they better let him win or lose on his own, fair and square, or they'd be arrested.

He and Hellen hid and watched as the hucksters gave Opie the good gun, and he hit 5 bullseyes and won the razor, which he gave to his dad as a birthday gift.

Opie never knew how Andy had taken all of that which was stacked against him, and allowed him to prosper.

It reminded me of how God does this for us.

Coffee and Prayers

There are those who talk about us behind our backs. They speak evil of us. They call us names; they plot against us and even poison others against us. They seek our misery at best, our destruction at worst.

God sees this. He knows this. Even when we don't know and don't see that which is working against us, HE DOES.

He will allow that which some plot against us to actually go against those who are plotting against us.

He knows the hearts of these people. He knows the evil that is within them.

God takes people and obstacles out of our way, most of the time without our knowledge. Scripture tells us this in Psalm 138:7
"Though I walk in the midst of trouble, You will revive me; You will stretch out Your hand Against the wrath of my enemies, And Your right hand will save me."

The enemy is always out there. He's always plotting our demise. There's always people out there speaking evil behind our backs.

Coffee and Prayers

From Genesis to Revelation, all through the Bible there have been those who are against God's people. Don't be concerned. It's not new. Even Jesus Himself had people plotting and scheming against Him, complaining about everything He did.

God sees this and He hears.

He's there to make a way for us. Have a great day everyone.

"Do not fret because of evildoers, Nor be envious of the workers of iniquity. For they shall soon be cut down like

the grass, And wither as the green herb. Trust in the Lord, and do good; Dwell in the land, and feed on His faithfulness. Delight yourself also in the Lord; And He shall give you the desires of your heart. Commit your way to the Lord; Trust also in Him, And He shall bring it to pass. He shall bring forth your righteousness as the light, And your justice as the noonday. Rest in the Lord, and wait patiently for Him; Do not fret because of him who prospers in his way, Because of the man who brings wicked schemes to pass. Cease from anger, and forsake wrath; Do not fret— it only causes harm. The wicked plots against the just, And gnashes at him with his teeth. The Lord laughs at him; For He sees that his day is coming. The wicked have drawn the sword And have bent their bow, To cast down the poor and needy, To slay those who are of upright conduct. Their sword shall enter their own heart, And their bows shall be broken." Psalm 37:1-8, 12-15

Coffee and Prayers this Friday Morning.

Yesterday was the 41st Anniversary of Elvis' death.

A few years ago on Elvis' birthday, someone made the remark to me "You sure know a lot about Elvis." That got me to thinking, as a lot of things usually do.

Yes I do know a lot about Elvis. I know his birthday, I know when he died. I know about his twin brother who died at birth. I know his parent's names. I know his grandmother's name. I know his daughter's name and when she was born. I know his ex-wife's name. I know most of his bodyguard's names. I know that he and his family moved to Memphis when he was young, and that he graduated from Humes High School. I know that he worked for Crown Electric driving a truck for $35 a week. I know that the man who discovered him when he came in to make a record for his mother was Sam Phillips. I know that the first house that Elvis bought was on Audubon Drive in Memphis. I know what year he bought Graceland and how much he paid for it and the acres around it. I could go on and on and on. Yes I know a lot ABOUT Elvis, but I didn't KNOW Elvis. I'm Facebook friends with one of his step-brothers, Rick Stanley. You see Rick KNEW Elvis, he didn't just know ABOUT him.

So how about the Lord? How many of us know ABOUT the Lord, but don't KNOW the Lord?

Yes we can read the Bible and know all ABOUT the Lord. We can read every word from Genesis to Revelation, and we can know ABOUT God. But what about KNOWING Him?

You see there is a difference don't you? It's like believing IN God and BELIEVING God. Many people believe IN God, they just don't BELIEVE God. They believe that He exists; they just don't believe Him when He says "I so love you that I gave my only Son for you."

We can get to KNOW God by praying to Him, talking to Him, and LISTENING to Him. We can get to KNOW Him by reading His word and praying that His word is made clear to us. We can get to KNOW

Coffee and Prayers

Him by accepting Him, and realizing that He loves us more than we could ever love ourselves or one another. We can know His heart, His will for us, His plan for us. When we know Him, we know that He will never allow anything to come against us that isn't filtered through His hands.

We can know ABOUT anyone by reading about them. We can KNOW a person by talking to them, learning their heart. We can know God by being on our faces to Him daily. He wants us to seek Him, and to KNOW Him, not just know ABOUT Him. When we get to KNOW Him, then we know that the lies of the enemy are just that; lies. When the Enemy tells us that we are not good enough for God; we KNOW that we are MADE good enough for God because Jesus makes us good enough when we are His.

We cannot accept just knowing ABOUT Him. We must KNOW Him. We can't accept just believing IN HIM, we must BELIEVE Him.

If you don't KNOW Him, then seek Him. He will make Himself known to you. He will answer. Seek Him diligently. He's not hiding.

So when someone says to you, "You know a lot about God", you can say "No, I don't know ABOUT God, I KNOW God."

Coffee and Prayers

Have a great day everyone. "Ask, and it will be given to you; seek, and you will find; knock, and it will be opened to you. For everyone who asks receives, and he who seeks finds, and to him who knocks it will be opened.'" Matthew 7:7-8

Coffee and Prayers this Cold Thanksgiving Morning.

I was thinking the other day about growing up in Terrace Gardens in Greenwood as a child. My parents had their first house built there.

It was among the first few houses built in the neighborhood back in those days. Ours, the Tumminello's, the Hankins, the Campbell's, and just a few more were the first ones built in what used to be a cotton field , and would , over the decades , become a large neighborhood.

Behind my house on Linden Street was a drainage ditch that all of us kids used to play in. We called it "The Ditch". Right near my house was a drain pipe, surrounded by concrete, where all of the rain water from the streets would empty into the ditch. This part of the ditch was our gathering place. There was always a huge pool of water there where the pipe emptied, and it always contained turtles, crawfish, and so on. This concrete surrounding the pipe was huge .It was our "base". As we played in and around the ditch, it was our go to place.

I remember many years later I decided to walk down there to that huge concrete drain pipe. As I stood there I couldn't believe it. It wasn't huge at all! It was quite small. The huge water hole was very small as well. What had changed? Me! I was grown now. My perspective had changed.

My view had changed.

I was mature, and could see it from a different angle.

I thought back on the dirt clod "fights", chase, hide and seek, and other games all of us kids played there. Had we ever been that small? Had the ditch ever been that huge?

Such is life. We have problems in life, and when we are going through them they look huge. They seem larger than life. It's when we don't look at our problems with God's perspective that they seem too large for us.

Is anything too hard for God? When we place our problems in His hands, we can look back later and say "Was my problem ever that big? Was I ever that small?" We tend to look at our problems with the wrong perspective. We look at them as if we are a child and very small. Wet end to not offer them to God, Who is bigger than any problem or any issue.

It's when we lay our problems at His feet that we can say "Lord, You are bigger than this. "When we lose our job, God is bigger. When our spouse says "I'm sorry, it's over." God is bigger. When the doctor says "There's nothing we can do", God is bigger. When the banker says "I'm sorry, there's nothing we can do", God is bigger. When our teenage kids or outgrown kids are living completely contrary to how we've raised them and acting as if they've lost their minds, God is bigger. We are getting nothing but "Hell by the acre", GOD IS BIGGER! Put it in HIS hands. Don't be as a little child looking at a huge ditch, look at it as a grown adult who has the Creator of the universe as your Savior. Keep praying, keep praying, and keep praying. God is bigger. He loves us and only wants what is best for us.

Have a Happy Thanksgiving everyone.

"'For My thoughts are not your thoughts,
Nor are your ways My ways,'" says the Lord.

Coffee and Prayers

'For as the heavens are higher than the earth,
So are My ways higher than your ways,
And My thoughts than your thoughts.'" Isaiah 55:8-9

Coffee and Prayers this Morning.

About 25 degrees warmer than just 24 hours ago.

Yesterday I was thinking about a story that I heard many years ago about a Texas oil millionaire named Duncan Brice. One morning he came downstairs and his son, Duncan Jr, who was about 25 at the time, was wearing a beautiful silver Stetson hat.

"Where did you get that hat?" Duncan Sr wanted to know. "Neiman Marcus" Duncan Jr replied. "Well I want one!" the elder Brice told him. "I will make all the arrangements Pop." His son replied.

Soon the elder Brice was in his limo and was met outside the Neiman Marcus location by several of the store staff. They escorted him inside, and had several different style Stetson hats from which to choose. After choosing his style, a big silver one like his son's, his head size was measured, and he was told that the hat would be custom fitted. He was brought into a room with a large comfortable chair, a large screen TV, and the was brought out ice tea and various other snacks that he requested. As several staff members brought him out items as he waited, he finally asked the woman in charge "Well what exactly is this going to cost me?" The woman replied "Well Mr. Brice, the hat is $8,000, and the custom fit is $2,000." Mr. Brice jumped up and exclaimed "Ten thousand dollars?? This is costing me ten thousand dollars?" This is outrageous!" After ranting for a few minutes the woman calmly said "Mr. Brice, I'm sorry, but your son Duncan Jr called and said that you wanted a hat exactly like the one that he had purchased."

"Well" The elder Brice said "Duncan Jr has a rich daddy, I DON'T!"

Do we often feel like the elder Mr. Brice? Do we feel like someone else is getting a blessing at our expense? We see those who seemingly never have a problem, never have serious "life issues" in which they have to deal with. Life for them always seems to have them coming out smelling like a rose, as the old saying goes.

When we feel that way, we are not seeing the big picture. We likely have those who are looking at us, envious of us. It's easy to celebrate the blessings of fellow Christians, it's hard, however, when we see those who are not Christians who seem to have it all in life.

We need to focus more on what we are being blessed with endless on what we see others blessed with, or what we perceive to be blessed with.

As I've said so many times, God uses timing, not time. That which we may think is working against us can sometimes actually work FOR US later down the road. That which we think is blessing someone may actually end up being a curse against them later down the road. We should focus our prayers on God giving us wisdom, and seek His will with our whole hearts. We should focus more on what God wants for us and seek that.

Ask for wisdom, dismiss the envy. It's hard to do no doubt. But when we do we can be much more content.

Have a great day everyone.

"But as for me, my feet had almost stumbled; my steps had nearly slipped. For I was envious of the boastful, when I saw the prosperity of the wicked. Behold, these are the ungodly, who are always at ease; they increase in riches. Surely I have cleansed my heart in vain, and washing my hands in innocence. For all day long I have been plagued, and chastened every morning. If I had said 'I will speak thus', Behold I would have been untrue to the generation of Your children. When I thought how to understand this, it was too painful for me- until I went into the sanctuary of God; Then I understood their end." Psalm 73:2-3- 12-17

Coffee and Prayers this Sunday Morning.

I was thinking about a story that was told, I believe, by comedian Jerry Clower years ago. His uncle Versy cut wood for a living, and used an axe and a cross cut saw. One day it was suggested to him that he could cut five times as much wood with a chain saw than he did with an axe and a cross cut saw. He decided to buy a chainsaw and try it. He returned the chainsaw a few days later. He was angry and upset that it took him now ten times as long, and didn't even cut half of the wood! The man at the store suggested that something was wrong with the saw, and cranked it. Uncle Versy jumped back and with a surprised look asked "What's that noise?" His uncle had no idea that you actually have to crank it to make it work right! Of course the story is most likely fiction, but hilarious because that's the way some people are about many things. They get frustrated with the way something doesn't work that they aren't using right.

That can be from a phone to a car to a computer to an appliance.

People are also that way with God as well. They wonder why life seems such a mess all the time. They never pray, they never read His word, they never once consider Him until they need a "wish list", such as they would with Santa Clause. They want a job, a house, a car, all their bills paid and all relationships fixed. But they never honor Him, never consider Him, only want Him in their lives, sort of like a fire extinguisher, just hanging there until needed.

They want a "relationship" with a "good man" or a "good woman", but look for these "good" people in places where good people don't hang out.

As a result, their lives are sorta like "Uncle Versy" was, trying to cut a tree down with a chainsaw that isn't even cranked. They have no idea what God says about our lives, our relationships, our marriages, our children, our finances, because they've never read God's instructions.

Coffee and Prayers

It's when we are in constant prayer, constantly in God's word, daily trying to draw closer to Him that we reap the benefits of His blessings and protection.

We can do much more when we honor Him, trust Him, and keep His words in our hearts. We can do much more when we ask and seek His will instead of our own. We won't be working ten times as hard for no results when we are in His will, His word. Have a great Lord's Day everyone.

"'Therefore do not worry, saying, 'What shall we eat?' or 'What shall we drink?' or 'What shall we wear?' For after all these things the Gentiles seek. For your heavenly Father knows that you need all these things. But seek first the kingdom of God and His righteousness, and all these things shall be added to you. Therefore do not worry about tomorrow, for tomorrow will worry about its own things. Sufficient for the day is its own trouble.'" Matthew 6:31-34

Coffee and Prayers this Freezing Cold, Wet, Miserable Morning.

I was thinking about this morning about how some people act when you first meet them. You are introduced to someone, they shake your hand and the first question out of their mouth is "So what do you do for a living?" It's as if they want to size you up and determine if you're "worth" their time or friendship. They want to see if there is maybe any way that you can be of service to them at some point. They place your worth to them in proportion to what you can do FOR them.

My first Manager at Coca-Cola used to really take people aback when they'd ask him that. When someone would ask what he does for a living, Gary would say "I'm in the banking business. I rob em!" That always made jaws drop!

I think one of the most important jobs in the world is a woman who is a "stay at home" wife and mother. Raising children, teaching them, caring for the home, is extremely important, and if a household can make it on one income, I think is great. I've seen people turn their nose up at stay at home moms.

I've seen people turn their nose up at anyone who they think is "beneath" them.

That's the way some people are. I've seen managers in the corporate world who wouldn't even look the person in the eye who empties the trash. I've seen them look down with disdain on

Coffee and Prayers

the person or people in the mail room. I've seen it so many times that a person just has no use for anyone that he or she doesn't consider an "equal" in income or importance.

Two of the best compliments I've ever received was one time years ago when the cleaning lady, an elderly black lady named Mandy , brought me a little gift on my birthday. She said "You always so nice to me, I just wanted to get you a little something." I was brought to tears. Another was a time when I was at Coca-Cola, one of the gate checkers who had been working there 35 years told me this one day just out of the blue as I stood down at the gate while waiting for some of my guys to get back.

He said "Billy, I've been here a lot of years. You're the first person I've ever met here who didn't become an (expletive deleted) when he became a manager!"

He went on to say that so many had been promoted and then thought that everyone else was beneath them.

How do we view those who are in no position to ever do anything for us? How does Jesus view us? What can we ever do for HIM? Yet He loves us more than we can ever imagine. Do we love and

Coffee and Prayers

respect those whose jobs we don't consider "important"? Do we look down upon the waiter and waitress who serves us? Do we look down upon anyone who we don't feel as equals? How many place the

Hollywood "stars" above the EMT? Above police, firemen, soldiers?

Who did Jesus die for? All of us. He reached out to the leper, the sick, the diseased, the woman caught in adultery, the thief on the cross next to Him.

Some will look at those in the Armani suits, the biggest, finest car, the title behind the name or in front of the name. They will look at the "social status" to judge. That's not how God sees us. He sees through what we have or don't have. He sees through all the walls we put up. He ignores all the filters we try to view ourselves and others through.

We may even look down upon ourselves at times. We may judge ourselves because of failures and circumstances that have left us bare.

Some judge themselves harsher than anyone else does. Fortunately for us, God looks at what we have INSIDE.

Coffee and Prayers

Let's all look deeper at one another. Have a great day everyone.

"'For the Lord does not see as man sees; for man looks at the outward appearance, but the Lord looks at the heart.'" 1 Sam 16:7

Coffee and Prayers this Cool Morning.

Much to do today.

Praying for peace for those who need it, strength for those who need it, and wisdom for us all. Life at times seems to be turned on its ear, then God starts to turn it back, even better than we could ever imagine just a few weeks ago.

As I was driving yesterday I heard a commercial for the Home Depot. It got me to thinking about how much "Do it yourself" is pushed these days. Just a Google search of "Do it yourself" will yield thousands of results from home projects to legal actions!

It made we wonder about how many people annually have a "Do it Yourself" turn into "I've done it" disaster.

Coffee and Prayers

Some projects require little skill, and can be learned watching a short video or by reading instructions.

But how many REALLY turn out like the picture on the box?

A salesman in a do it yourself store will make you believe that you can tile a floor quite easily. That's their job to make you feel that you can do it.

Laying a tile floor is a lot more complicated than it is always made out to be. Ask anyone who has done it on their own. Now some have good results, but many have a disaster. And if it's a "DIY", you own it so you've wasted your time and your money. A few dollars spent on a skilled, experienced contractor, or whoever can make a world of difference.

And anyone can tell you that ANYTHING worth doing is worth doing right, and it's easier to do it right the first time than to try to do over.

But those big stores make it sound so EASY to do yourself.

That's how it is in life sometimes. People will try to work out everything on their own. They feel that they can handle any situation as a "do it yourself".

Coffee and Prayers

They don't seek wisdom of those who are skilled and / or experienced in life matters.

Or, they listen to those who have made a mess of things over and over again.

The devil wants us to be a "does it yourself" society. He will tell you that you don't need God for your life choices.

"You don't need God, if you want that man, leave your husband and get him." "Don't want your wife? Just dump her and go for that one you do want." Don't read God's word. You can afford it. That's what credit cards are for. Max'em out." That's what Satan tells people. "Christian counsel? Who needs that? Live the way YOU want to. Don't listen to them; just do what you want to do."

The devil will sell us a bill of goods if we let him. He will convince us that we can do it. Just as long as it is not within God's will then it's okay.

Just as with a home project or any other similar thing, the unskilled can find him or herself in a huge mess.

Do it our "own way" will lead us to say "Uh oh, I should have done this first", or "I left out a step", or "I did this backwards."

Coffee and Prayers

Life, like a project, can become a disaster.

Instructions on so many things read "For best results ____".

If we want "best results", we need to stay on our face, seeking His will, stay in His Word, living as we should. We should also seek counsel from wise, Godly Christians.

Want a joyous, happy, fulfilled Christian marriage? Then seek the counsel of a Christian couple. Want to live a Christian life? Seek counsel from those who live one. Want financial security? Seek counsel from those who manage their finances well.

If your life is already a "do it yourself" disaster, it can ALWAYS, ALWAYS be remade. God is the ultimate contractor. He can fix a life, He can fix people, He can fix relationships, He can cure addictions, He can repair what is broken. He can and will put on your heart who it is you need to seek wisdom from.

There will be things that we must do, often painful things. We may have to painfully rip out so much of the old that we think that it may never be right again.

Coffee and Prayers

But eventually, there will be that finished result. That "best result". Seek HIM. Don't trust in your own "understanding".

Ask Him.

He can do it, and the devil can't help.

Have a great day everyone.

"You lust and do not have. You murder and covet and cannot obtain. You fight and war. Yet you do not have because you do not ask. You ask and do not receive, because you ask amiss, that you may spend it on your pleasures." James 4:2-3

Coffee and Prayers this Snow and Ice Covered Thursday.

Forty degrees colder than what it was just 24 hours ago. I posted this a couple of years ago and was reminded of it again yesterday.

I saw some Easter candy in a store yesterday and it reminded me of something that happened a few years ago. I was in Tractor Supply Company in Batesville a week or so before Easter. They had

Coffee and Prayers

baby ducks and chicks there in metal tubs on the floor. A little boy, maybe 6 or 7 years old was looking over into the tub with the chicks and he began to yell at them.

People were looking at him with anger on their faces.

His mother ran over and grabbed him by the arm "What are you doing?" She asked as she bent down, still holding his arm "Have you lost your mind?" The little boy innocently looked at her and said "I was giving a shout to my peeps!"

Well I lost it! I fell out laughing!

This kid had as warped a sense of humor as I have apparently.

As his mother angrily dragged him away, he looked at me with an impish grin as if to say "Thank you for understanding." I "got it", only because of my sense of humor I suppose.

This kid wasn't being bratty; he was trying to be funny. I thought it hilarious, and his mom shot me an angry look as if to say "Don't encourage him!"

Isn't it that way in everyday life? We see people but not their hearts.

Coffee and Prayers

That person who cuts us off in traffic, we see them as a jerk, but what if something is just on their heart that has them distracted so that they didn't even sees us? What is truly going on with them?

That person who walked out and didn't hold the door for you? Maybe his or her heart is hurting, and they aren't thinking. It doesn't make them a bad person. We just don't see what's going on. We don't know their story.

What if their wife or husband just filed for divorce?

Suppose they have a sick child or parent? Suppose they just received a bad report from the doctor? Suppose they just got a layoff notice?

We only see how it affects US, no matter what someone's actions are.

We are too busy many times to care. Do we notice the countenance of a stranger? Do we see the hurt in their eyes?

We don't know what they are facing. Do we give the understanding that we would want to receive? Do we sometimes have those times when OUR issues in life may cause us to be uncharacteristically rude or aloof? Of course we do.

Coffee and Prayers

Many people just are distracted by life issues. It doesn't always mean that they are a jerk, although they may be. In either case, they need our prayers.

Just as that little boy, we can all be misunderstood for a variety of reasons.

Let's not judge by the outside appearances. We don't know the internal battles others may be facing. Let's try to take our blinders off when it comes to others when we only see a fraction of a second of them. They all have a story. They all have a struggle. Let's keep one another prayed up.

Have a great day everyone.

"By this we know love, because He laid down His life for us. And we also ought to lay down our lives for the brethren. But whoever has this world's goods, and sees his brother in need, and shuts up his heart from him, how does the love of God abide in him? My little children, let us not love in word or in tongue, but indeed and in truth. And by this we know that we are of the truth, and shall assure our hearts before Him. For if our heart condemns us, God is greater than our heart, and knows all things. Beloved, if our heart does not condemn us, we have confidence toward God. And whatever we ask we receive from Him, because we keep His commandments and do those things that are pleasing in His sight. And this is His commandment: that we should believe on the name of His Son Jesus Christ and love one another, as He gave us commandment." 1 John 3:16-23

Coffee and Prayers this Much Cooler Friday Morning.

It feels like this week has been a month long.

Yesterday I was thinking about what an army buddy told all of us one day about when he was in Basic Combat Training at Ft Jackson SC in 1981. There was a guy in his platoon (can't remember his name) who was a Cherokee Indian. He was small in stature, about 5'7" he said.

The first few days of Basic Training saw this proud Cherokee become the brunt of jokes and racial slurs. White and black alike kept making jokes at his expense.

After a few days of this, he stood up one day and walked to the barracks door. With an extremely loud "Kiai!!!" he jumped straight up and kicked the top of the door frame. His kick was so powerful that it cracked the door frame. He never said another word. He simply turned around and looked at the other soldiers. They all stood there, mouths wide open in astonishment.

My friend said that no one else ever picked on that small but powerful and proud Cherokee again.

Life can be like that. We get attacked by the enemy daily. We have the devil accusing us, throwing our past up in our faces, and constantly telling us how small we are. He disparages us by mocking our Christianity.

Sometimes, we have to simply show our strength and power to him. Not ours on our own, because we are helpless .We have to show our power through Christ Jesus. We have to show that His blood covers us.

The enemy will take any and all opportunity to kill, steal, and destroy. He will use anything and everything he can against us.

A show of power to him is all that it takes to show that you, through Christ, are powerful enough to defeat anything the enemy lines up to attack you with.

Staying on our faces to Him, seeking His will, and staying in His word can do this. Those lonely nights when we are under attack, walking the floors and citing the Bible aloud will make the enemy flee. He cannot stand to hear us reciting God's word. He cannot stand to hear truth, and he cannot stand to hear us declare that Jesus is Lord, He is our King, and He is our Savior. The enemy knows that he has no power over us when we are a child of God.

If you are being attacked and accused by the enemy, then show your strength. Declare to the enemy loudly and defiantly that God does battle for us, and that NO WEAPON FORMED AGAINST US SHALL PROSPER!

Kick that door facing, so to speak, and make your power through HIM be known.

Have a great day everyone.

"For they intended evil against You;
They devised a plot which they are not able to perform.
Therefore You will make them turn their back;
You will make ready Your arrows on Your string toward their faces.
Be exalted, O Lord, in Your own strength!
We will sing and praise Your power." Psalm 21:11-13

Coffee and Prayers

Coffee and Prayers this Thursday Morning.

A couple of years ago, Cindy wanted me to watch "Anne of Green Gables" with her. I had never seen it, nor had I read the book growing up. I've read most of the classics as a child such as "The Swiss Family Robinson," "Born Free," "The Call of the Wind," and others, but I had never seen it or read it.

The story is about Anne Shirley, a 12-year-old orphan. When a middle-aged brother and sister, Mirilla and Matthew, send for an orphan boy to help with their farm, they are instead sent Anne. She immediately grows on Matthew when he first meets her, Mirilla takes a little longer.

One day, Mirilla angrily asks Anne if she had taken her beloved brooch. Anne admits that she admired it, but insists that she immediately returned it.

The brooch cannot be found. Mirilla threatens to send her back to the orphanage and confines her to her room until she confesses to taking it.

Finally, Anne tells Mirilla that she took it and was pretending to be Lady Fitzgerald and the brooch had slipped from her hand and fallen into the lake. Anne's confession was detailed and extensive.

Coffee and Prayers

Anne was confined to her room, and now afraid she'd be sent back.

As Mirilla is putting on her shawl to go somewhere, Matthew notices something dangling from the shawl. It is Mirilla's brooch. It had gotten snagged on her shawl. Mirilla is perplexed. She goes to Anne's room and asks her why she made up such an elaborate confession (a lie) when she knew she was innocent. Anne replies, "Because you wouldn't believe the truth."

What a stinging thing, isn't it?

When we speak the truth and it isn't believed, it is a hurt that just hurts down to one's very bones. While the movie is 30 years old, the novel is over 100 years old, rejection of truth is as old as time itself. We have all had the truth rejected. Not even God Himself is immune to having His truth rejected. The very first man and woman rejected God's truth. And of course, ever since, the world has known sin. Jesus had His truth rejected by many as well. This happens on a daily basis and has tens of millions of times since Eve first believed Satan's lie, "You will NOT surely die!" God had given Adam and Even His rule. Only ONE RULE! He told them that they could eat of any tree in the garden except one. God walked with them in the cool of the day, every day. He showed His love to them, and then one day Satan, whose only purpose is to kill, steal, and destroy, tells Eve that God is a liar. Eve rejects the truth for a lie, and Adam does as well.

The VERY FIRST institution that Satan attacked with his lies was marriage (family). He is still doing it today. And it's getting worse.

The result is what you see in the news every day. What you read in the history books and what we read in the Bible. I think maybe if we asked Jesus, "Why did You have to be crucified, die, and rise again," He could very well say what Anne said, "Because you wouldn't believe the TRUTH!"

Jesus has never nor will He ever replace the truth with a lie. That's what Satan does. Jesus wants to give us a life more abundant.

Things are NOT always as they appear to be, God always has a purpose in what He does.

Sin keeps us a prisoner. Lies of the enemy keeps us a prisoner.

The TRUTH sets us free. (John 8:32) Anything contradictory to God's word is a lie. Have a great day everyone.

Coffee and Prayers

"'The thief does not come except to steal, and to kill, and to destroy. I have come that they may have life and that they may have it more abundantly.'" John 10:10

Coffee and Prayers this Tuesday Morning.

I was flipping channels Sunday and passed the movie "The Karate Kid." In the movie, Daniel Larusso and his widowed mother move from New Jersey to California. Daniel begins to be bullied by a group of bullies who are karate experts known as the "Cobra Kai's." The handyman in Daniel's apartment complex is an old man from Okinawa named Mr. Miagi.

Miagi agrees to teach Daniel karate for self-defense IF Daniel agrees to do exactly what Miagi says. Starting with washing Miagi's 20 or so old cars and waxing them in a certain way. Left hand "wax on," right hand "wax off." Then, he had to paint the fence a certain way, the house a certain way, and sand the complex deck a certain way. Daniel then became angry because Miagi had not taught him ANYTHING over these few weeks. Of course, it turns out that the hand movements used to wax on, wax off, paint, etcetera, were part of his training. When Daniel realized this, he realized that all of that which made no sense at the time now made perfect sense. He would then go on to win the "All Valley" karate tournament, which the Cobra Kai had dominated for years, thus also winning their respect.

That's the way it is with God at times, isn't it? He has us to do things that, at the time, make no sense at all. Then we find out later that it all made perfect sense. He was using HIS WAY. The best way. It didn't seem to make sense for Noah to build an Ark for 120 years, where there was no water and there had never been any of this "rain" on earth. It didn't make any sense for Moses to go before Pharoah, the most powerful leader on earth at that time, and demand the freedom of the Hebrew slaves with nothing more than a stick in his hand.

It didn't make sense for the freed slaves, Israel, to wander the desert for 40 years when they could have been in the promised land in a couple of weeks. Many, many examples of God instructing someone to do something that made no sense are all throughout the Bible. They make no sense to man, but perfect sense to God.

Many things my parents taught me as a child made no sense to me then, but I use them daily now.

Coffee and Prayers

Many things I learned in basic combat training made no sense then, but I use them to this day.

We will not always understand immediately what God is doing through us. There were times when I've been on my face before God and I've confessed that I was confused, hurt, and feeling lost and alone, but I trusted Him in whatever He was doing. Even when it made no sense. My main emphasis was "Lord, don't let me miss the message in all this."

What is He telling you that seems to be pointless? Senseless? Are you trusting your own understanding or His might and power and wisdom? As I've said before, it's like my friend Doug Walker says, "He's either working something into you or out of you." It may not ever make perfect sense to you, this side of heaven, but when it's filtered through God's hands, then it's perfect for us. Don't be discouraged. It won't make sense always. Just have faith in HIM. Have a great day everyone.

"Though the fig tree may not blossom, Nor fruit be on the vines; Though the labor of the olive may fail, And the fields yield no food; Though the flock may be cut off from the fold, And there be no herd in the stalls— Yet I will rejoice in the Lord, I will joy in the God of my salvation. The Lord God is my had to be that way. Who was to blame for his crucifixion? We all are. As I said, it was not just the physical pain. There were many others who were crucified in those days. He was crucified between two thieves that day. The physical pain, the worst pain ever conceived, failed in comparison to the emotional pain He suffered.

The spiritual pain.

There He was, completely innocent, the only person who was ever without sin, yet He was now guilty. Every murder, rape, robbery, every vile sin you could imagine, He was now guilty of. He bore our shame. God the Father could no longer look upon Him and had to look away. For the first time ever, He was alone. God the Father was, at that moment, no longer with him. It caused Him to cry out, "Eli, Eli, lama sabachthani?" that is, "My God, My God, why have You forsaken me?" God the Father could not look upon this sin that was now upon Him. His death, burial, and resurrection saved us all who accept Him and believe in Him.

Think about His disciples. What were they feeling?

The future looked dark. He had been tortured, crucified, died, and placed in the tomb. What had happened? They were confused. They didn't understand. After all He had said and done, was it over now? What would be next? But then they came to the tomb and it was empty. The stone had been rolled away. Not to let Him out, but to show that He is risen. He lives, and as He lives, so shall we live forever with Him if we are His. Scripture records it this way; Luke 24:1-8 Now on the first day of the week, very early in the morning, they, and certain other women with them, came to the tomb bringing the spices which they had prepared. But they found the stone rolled away from the tomb. Then they went in and did not find the body of the Lord Jesus. And it happened, as they were greatly perplexed about this, that behold, two men stood by them in shining garments.

Then, as they were afraid and bowed their faces to the earth, they said to them, "Why do you seek the living among the dead? He is not here, but is risen! Remember how He spoke to you when He was still in Galilee, saying, 'The Son of Man must be delivered into the hands of sinful men, and be crucified, and the third day rise again.'" And they remembered His words.

He is not a God of the past, He is a God of the present, and works in our lives right now. As I watched the scenes of His brutal punishment and being nailed to the cross, I thought, "That is what I DESERVE." Yet He took it for me. It was never meant for me to take it. He settled it for me, for us, long ago. He said on the cross "It is finished."

And it is. Have a great Resurrection Day everyone. "He made Him who knew no sin on our behalf, that we might become the righteousness of God in Him." 2 Corinthians 5:21

Coffee and Prayers this Rainy Sunday Morning.

Was thinking as I watch Fox News and the conversation surrounding the Sandy Hook School shooting. I was watching about how several years ago at a family gathering, someone was talking about her son, who was about 8 or 9 years old. She was saying that he will not pay attention in school, will not mind at home, and listed a number of 'disorders' that he had. My then father-in-law said, "They had a CURE for that when I was growing up."

Amen to that.

Yesterday at the funeral, my best friend Robbie and I were talking with a friend that had grown up with us. His Mom had even been a teacher of ours. We were discussing how Bible stories were read to us back then at Davis Elementary, and how if we

Coffee and Prayers

became disruptive in class we were medicated. We were given a dose of wood, applied liberally to our rear ends. It was given on an 'as needed' basis. Needless to say, there was not a lot of us who needed it. Not repeatedly anyway.

It was the same way at home. We were not allowed to "get away" with what is gotten away with these days.

As the '90s rolled around, it seemed like discipline was replaced with medicine. I began to more and more children being on some type of behavior modification meds. I am not, nor will I pretend to be an expert on the subject, but it seems to me that we are now an over-medicated society.

I pray that I do not offend anyone whose child truly needs medication, it is just in my heart that it seems to have taken the place of discipline.

It just seems that boys and girls are just being boys and girls, and when they cross a line in their behavior, they aren't being reigned in and taught what is acceptable and what isn't. They are simply being medicated. Have we, as a society, lost the will or simply can't take the time to modify behavior by other means?

Honestly, I don't know. I cannot answer to that to which I don't know. I can only comment on what God places on my heart.

I do know that I see more and more children trained on medication rather than by Biblical discipline. These children have become front-page headlines in Columbine and Sandy Hook as well as numerous other places. All I can say is that the Bible works. Every time it is tried. We need to go back and read the instructions.

Have a great Lord's Day.

"He who spares the rod hates his son, but he who loves him disciplines him promptly." Proverbs 13:24

Coffee and Prayers this Wednesday Morning.

The other day, I saw a DVD for the television show "The Big Valley." It was always one of my favorite TV westerns. The show centers around the Barkley family. A wealthy family in Stockton, California, set in the 1870s. The family is led by the matriarch, Victoria Barkley. Her husband, Tom, had been killed in a range war. They are wealthy, having a huge ranch, cattle, mining, and farming operations.

Coffee and Prayers

There is soft-spoken Jarod, the oldest, who is an attorney, Nick, who runs the ranch and other operations and would as soon punch someone as look at them, Audra, their beautiful sister, and youngest brother, Eugene, who was written out of the series the second season.

In the pilot episode, a young man named Heath shows up. He claims that he is the son of Tom Barkley. Heath's motherhood told him on her death bed who his father was. Tom had met Heath's mother when he was checking on one of their mines in the tiny town of Strawberry. Heath's story would check out, and Heath was accepted into the family. Victoria would call Heath her son, and care for him though not one drop of her blood was in him. And it hurt her deeply that her late husband had been unfaithful. Nick, Jarod, and Audra called Heath their brother.

He would sweat, fight, and bleed for the Barkley name and their empire alongside him.

Then one day a man named Charlie Sawyer shows up. He claims that he was married to Heath's mother and was his real father. Sawyer is a con man and he's running from men he's swindled.

This news isn't readily accepted by any of the Barkleys. Heath rides to Strawberry to see if

Coffee and Prayers

anyone remembers Sawyer. Hanna, the old black lady who helped raise Heath, and now whose memory is shaky at best, does remember him being married to Heath's mother.

Heath then decides to leave the Barkleys, since he's not one. Nick tries to tell him that he's their brother. Jarod tells Heath that he can make the Barkley name Heath's, legal as any birth certificate. Victoria, who considers Heath her son, is devastated that he wants to leave. She passionately tells Heath that he is a Barkley, if not by blood, then by love. She begs him to stay. She then yells at him, "You may walk out of here, but wherever you go and whatever you do, you will always be a BARKLEY!"

A few miles away as Heath has ridden off, he hears shots. Sawyer is shot while running from those men. Heath gets him back to the ranch, and Sawyer admits before he dies that he's not Heath's father, that he'd abandoned Heath's mother 2 years before Heath was born.

Heath's place in the Barkley family was secure. Even though he wasn't Victoria's blood son, she accepted him and loved him as her own. Heath's brothers and sister loved him and he them, despite the circumstances he was born in.

Yes, this is a fictional TV show, but I have a point.

All of that to say this. Blood doesn't always make family. Love makes the family. Loyalty makes the family. So much more makes the family than just "blood."

There are many, many people who have adopted children and even though they may not be "blood," they are their children, and the love couldn't be any stronger if there was blood. Many "step-parents" and "step-children" are not even referred to as "step." They are simply children. Because of love, not "blood." That's the way it should always be but isn't always.

So how are we in the family of Christ? It's because of blood. It's the blood of Christ.

Now just as Sawyer did with Heath, the devil will try to con us into thinking that we aren't truly a child of God. He will try to convince us and others that we aren't a true heir to salvation.
He will consistently and continually throw the past up to us. No matter how many times we fail or succeed, he will try to persuade us that we don't belong. Our past doesn't matter to Christ. That's why He shed His blood on the cross for us. Heath was a Barkley both by blood and by love. He was

accepted as their own, even if it had been that he wasn't by blood, he was one of them.

There is nothing we can do to make Jesus love us more. There is nothing that we've done that can make Him reject us when we come to Him. Never let the great con artist, the devil, or anyone else come in and try to convince you that you aren't a child of God.

Once we accept Him, we are His.

Have a great day everyone.

"But when the fullness of the time had come, God sent forth His Son, born of a woman, born under the law, to redeem those who were under the law, that we might receive the adoption as sons. And because you are sons, God has sent forth the Spirit of His Son into your hearts, crying out, 'Abba, Father!' Therefore you are no longer a slave but a son, and if a son, then an heir of God through Christ." Galatians 4:4-7

Coffee and Prayers this Thursday Morning.

Actually, this coffee is the most disgusting flavor I've ever had. It's got a "vanilla" flavor to it. I think we may have accidentally gotten a flavored creamer.

The other day I was watching a video on a police officer's site.

It was a confrontation between a police officer and a "free-inhabitant."

These so-called "free-inhabitants" are becoming more and more prevalent.

These "free-inhabitants" believe that they are free to do whatever they want without repercussions from the law whatsoever. They always cite the Articles of Confederation and misinterpret the law under these old articles that they think gives them the right to and privilege of living in the United States without having to follow any laws.

They drive vehicles without obtaining a driver's license. They do not get insurance and they feel as if they have the right to ignore any police officer's orders. To put it simply, they believe that the law does not apply to them. In fact, just a couple of years ago a woman and her family moved into an empty house in Memphis. She believed that it was her right to live there even though the house did not belong to her.

These people use a misinterpreted article in a law that is no longer valid in the United States to try to make others believe that they can live exactly as they want to without responsibilities whatsoever. They want every right and privilege given under the law without having to follow any law themselves.

And yes, being a student of government and history I understand that the old Articles of Confederation were never technically repealed. I do, however, know that the United States Confederation supersedes the old articles.

These people always do exactly as they want to do. But then, they run across a police officer who catches them breaking the law. It is their mistaken belief that they cannot be arrested because they are not subject to the law. It is often a hard and painful lesson for them to learn.

It does not matter whether or not they try to use this as an excuse, or if they sincerely believe that they are right. When they go before a judge, it isn't going to matter. They are subject to the law just as anyone else is. It doesn't matter what their sincerely held beliefs are.

Coffee and Prayers

Over this entire planet that we call earth, we have millions and millions of people who may not call themselves "free-inhabitant," but they live their lives in much the same way when it comes to God's laws.

They enjoy the air that God put into their lungs, just as believers do. The rain waters their crops just as it does the believers.

Just as many people live their lives as if there is no law, many more people live their lives as if there is no God.

I believe that these so-called "free-inhabitants," the vast majority of them, know full well that what they try to get by with is wrong, and they know it isn't legal. They just are too irresponsible to live within the law and think that if a day comes when they are confronted with a law enforcement officer or judge that they can bluff their way out of any charges.

It is also my belief that the vast majority of "atheists" know in their hearts that there is a God. They simply want to live as if He does not exist. They are too attached to sin to live in any other way.

One day, there will be a judgment. And those who have chosen to live as if there is no God, no judgment, will face a grim sentence. I think that those seven words, "Depart from me, I never knew you," are about the most tragic words anyone could ever hear.

Had it not been for my advocate, my Savior Jesus, paying for my sins on the cross, I too, would hear those words.

What about you? Are you living as if there is no law, no judgment? Or will you stand blameless, because it's all been paid for? If you haven't done so, accept Him as your Lord and Savior.

Have a great day everyone.

"Then I saw a great white throne and Him who sat on it, from whose face the earth and the heaven fled away. And there was found no place for them. And I saw the dead, small and great, standing before God, and books were opened. And another book was opened, which is the Book of Life. And the dead were judged according to their works, by the things which were written in the books. The sea gave up the dead who were in it, and Death and Hades delivered up the dead who were in them. And they were judged, each one according to his works. Then Death and Hades were cast into the lake of fire. This is the second death. And anyone not found written in the Book of Life was cast into the lake of fire." Revelation 20:11-15

Coffee and Prayers this Friday Morning.

The mystery of the awful coffee was cleaned up yesterday. Cindy had accidentally put hazelnut creamer in our creamer, but she removed it, now all is well with the world. As far as coffee that is.

One morning Colonel Cole, the Chief of Staff, was paying a visit to our unit. (The Chief of Staff is the "right-hand man" to the Adjutant General). Colonel Cole was a super nice guy. He looked the part of a Colonel, and in fact looked just like "central casting" had picked him for the part.

We had a large 30 cup coffee urn, and Colonel Cole was trying to get a cup of coffee, the last cup, from the urn. He was tilting the urn towards himself, trying to turn the spout and hold the cup. He glanced over at one of our men, a little sergeant named Larkins. Now Larkins was a good guy, a good soldier, extremely introverted and quiet. He stood there, arms folded, just watching Colonel Cole struggle. Colonel Cole glanced at Larkins and

Coffee and Prayers

asked "Well am I going to have to hold my cup, tilt the pot and hold open the spigot all at the same time?" Without a second's hesitation, Larkins replied "That's the way I had to do it sir", and walked off! As several of us had to walk off, about to bust a gut laughing, our Sergeant Major jumped into action to help the Colonel.

Life can be like that at times, and of course much more complicated than a cup of coffee. We have struggles and it seems that everyone else is just standing around watching, just happy that it's not them.

How do we help others when it seems that we are helpless to do so? All that we can do at times is just let them know we are there, are praying for them, and that they aren't alone. Life is full of mountains and valleys. And many times it seems like we are going through those valleys alone. And when we get to the mountain top we want to forget about those in their valleys. Maybe we can jump in and lend a hand. Maybe we can only pray for that person, that family in their situation. Their son is addicted? Do we just thank the Lord it isn't our son? Or do we sit in judgment? Their teen daughter is pregnant? What do we do for them? Judge and thank God it's not OUR daughter, or lift them up in prayers? We see someone lose their job, are we thankful it's not us, or do we pray for them and do all we can for them? It's easy to just stand there, knowing we've "had our coffee", and just watch others struggle. We have to take our blinders off to what others are going through.

I wish that I was guiltless in this, but it's very easy to get distracted by our own lives and forget the struggles of others. I certainly need to improve in this and will pray that God opens my eyes in this. We will all struggle at some point.

But we should pray with and for others, be glad for them when they achieve something, and be sympathetic and empathetic to everyone. I know that I've been prayed for when I struggled in every area of life. And I will make a concerted effort to do the same for others.

By the same token, we should not be envious of those who seem to have it "all together." We don't know what they struggle with or against.

Let's all lift one another up, let's pray for one another. Let's stay strong and keep the faith. Have a great day everyone.

"Let love be without hypocrisy. Abhor what is evil. Cling to what is good. Be kindly affectionate to one another with brotherly love, in honor giving preference to one another; not lagging in diligence, fervent in spirit, serving the Lord; rejoicing in hope, patient in tribulation, continuing steadfastly in prayer; distributing to the needs of the saints, given to hospitality. Bless those who persecute you; bless and do not curse. Rejoice with those who rejoice, and weep with those who weep. Be of the same mind toward one another. Do not set your mind on high things, but associate with the humble. Do not be wise in your own opinion. Repay no one evil for evil. Have regard for good things in the sight of all men. If it is possible, as much as depends on you, live peaceably with all men. Beloved, do not avenge yourselves, but rather give place to wrath; for it is written, "Vengeance is Mine, I will repay," says the Lord. Therefore "If your enemy is hungry, feed him; If he is thirsty, give him a drink; For in so doing you will heap coals of fire on his head." Do not be overcome by evil, but overcome evil with good." Romans 12:9-21

Coffee and Prayers this Saturday Morning.

I've posted this several times in the past. I think this was my friend Glenn's favorite post. I repost it in his honor today. I hope that it may help those who may be struggling with something this morning.

Coffee and Prayers

The other night as I was on patrol, I ran across our campus cat. I don't know her name, but she even has her own bed inside a room here, and she will let us know when she wants in to eat.

Whoever is in charge of her has a tiny bell attached to her collar. This is an attempt to keep her from killing birds and other small animals, as the bell will alert them to her presence.

Now God created the common cat to be a perfect killer. The cat is virtually silent. They have excellent night vision, an excellent sense of smell, and incredibly keen hearing. They approach their prey with total stealth, then spring upon them and kill with their powerful jaws and extremely sharp teeth.

People, however, will put a bell on a cat to keep it from killing birds and other small mammals. When they do this, they are taking away the cat's main weapon, which is stealth. A ringing bell prevents the cat from sneaking up on its prey and killing it.

It totally keeps the cat from what it was created to do.

I was thinking about how Satan does that to us. He hangs things around OUR necks to prevent us from doing what God created us to do.

Coffee and Prayers

Satan will hang guilt, shame, our past, remorse, pride, prejudice, regret, addiction, and anything else that he can upon us to keep us from being who and what God designed us to be and do.
We feel that we cannot be a help to anyone else because of our past. We feel that we cannot serve in our church because of our guilt or shame over a divorce, bankruptcy, a pregnant teen, or an addicted family member. He puts these "bells" on us that work not to alert others, but to try and constantly remind us of our past failings. It is meant to keep us from being who God shaped us to be.

Just as that bell on the cat's collar keeps her from being what God meant her to be, what Satan hangs on us does the same thing to us. Now the cat still is a cat, she looks the exact same, acts the exact same, and so forth, but she cannot fully be what she was created to be as long as she cannot hunt or kill as God designed her. That is fine for a cat, as long as the cat is being fed by someone. We, however, are meant to be so much more. We were bought and paid for with a price. We were paid for with Christ's blood. We were not meant to ever exist with that "bell" reminding us of what we once did, what we once were.

Coffee and Prayers

We are all new creatures when we are redeemed. Not perfect, but new. We cannot live with that "bell" of a failed marriage, failed finances, or children who act in a way completely contrary to the way that we raised them. We cannot live to our fullest with Satan's reminders constantly ringing in our ears. We were not meant to.

Take that bell off TODAY. Don't let anything or anyone tell you that you aren't good enough. Don't let the past hinder your future.

We were all meant for so much more. We can serve God and His people in the way that we were shaped, the way we were gifted when we listen to HIM.

Take off the negative "bells" that not only the devil hangs on you, but more often PEOPLE will hang on you. People want to relate you to your past. They only want to point a finger and say, "She used to..." or "I remember when he..."

God relates you to your future. He sent His Son to die for our sins and He never digs them up to use against us. Ever.

Take off that "bell" and put on what God gives you to make you that person He created you to be.

Coffee and Prayers

Stop listening to the lies of the enemy about yourself.

So what if you went through a divorce? So what if your teen is pregnant? So what if you had an addiction or are battling one now? Whatever your past is, SO WHAT?

It is up to GOD how He uses you.

Your worth is from God, not from people, and certainly not from the devil.

Have a great day everyone.

"The thief does not come except to steal, and to kill, and to destroy. I have come that they may have life and that they may have it more abundantly." John 10:10

Coffee and Prayers this Saturday Morning.

I was thinking about a story that I heard a long time ago. A little boy about 10 years old was looking around under a street light early one evening. A man approached and asked the boy what he was doing. The boy told him that he was looking for the silver dollar that he'd lost. The man began to help him look. After several minutes, the man asked him

Coffee and Prayers

where exactly he had been standing when he dropped the coin. The boy pointed across the street and said, "Down there, across the street." The man was incredulous. "Then why are you over here looking?" he asked. "Because the light is better over here," the boy replied.

Yes, it's a joke, but that's about the way some people are. They look for things in the wrong places. They look for happiness instead of joy. And they look for this happiness
in the wrong place. A bigger house, a better car, more money. All of that they think will fill the void in their life.

They want to find "Mr. Right" or "Mrs. Right." But they are looking in the wrong places.

Some men want to find a woman to share a life with. They search the bars and honky-tonks and juke joints and think she will be there. Women think that they will find their perfect man in the same place. They try it over and over and keep getting the same results. They keep following the wrong ones.

Meanwhile, that "Mr. Right," who is raising his small children alone is in church Sunday morning. He's not nursing a hangover. He spent his Saturday night on the couch watching movies with his kids.

Coffee and Prayers

That "Mrs. Right" is busy Sunday morning preparing her kids for church. She also spent Saturday night with her kids. She looks around church for her "Mr. Right." He looks around church for his "Mrs. Right."

Someone else is shopping for something to make their life better. They search for "happiness" under the street light while their "coin" is across the street.

Where are you looking? Do you have "happiness?" Because happiness depends on "happenings." Joy. True joy is found in the Lord. The Bible says in Nehemiah 8:10 Then he said to them, "Go your own, eat the fat, drink the sweet, and send portions to those for whom nothing is prepared; for this day is holy to our Lord. Do not sorrow, for the joy of the Lord is your strength."

Is the joy of the Lord YOUR strength? Or is it somewhere else?

One day, that man whose joy is in the Lord, who is raising kids alone, keeping them and himself in church, will meet that woman who is doing the same thing.

That person who thinks that a new car or other new "toys" will bring them joy may eventually learn that true joy comes from Him. They will see that being satisfied with the Lord will make their soul satisfied with everything else. They will see that as their praisings go up, His blessings will come down.

Are you searching for joy across the street and under the light such as that little boy? Or will you search where it can actually be found? Do you know that joy of the Lord already?

Have a great day everyone.

"But seek first the kingdom of God and His righteousness, and all these things shall be added to you." Matthew 6:33

Coffee and Prayers this Wednesday Morning.

The week is really dragging.

My house, being about 25 years old, tends to creak and pop as most houses do. I barely notice the sounds any longer. However, there are many times at night when I've been awakened by a noise that just didn't sound right. I will grab my weapon and clear every room before I can go back to sleep. I do a perimeter check around the outside. I make sure

Coffee and Prayers

all is ok before I go back to sleep. I won't rest until I make sure that noise that didn't sound right is checked out.

With so many preachers and evangelists on TV and radio, I like to make sure that when I hear something from one that "doesn't sound right"; I check it out with my other weapon, my Bible. A few months ago, I was listening to a local pastor on the radio. He was teaching that our salvation can be lost! I stopped listening immediately. I know better. I have God's word.

There are many verses, but John 10:29-30 sums it up best. "My Father, who has given them to Me, is greater than all; and no one is able to snatch them out of My Father's hand. I and My Father are one."

If Satan could steal the saved by taking their salvation, do you think there would be one saved person? If he could take one, he could and would take all.

I've even heard one well known, internationally famous "evangelist" spreading the doctrine of "chrislam", the supposed blending of Christianity and Islam. Look it up. It's one of the most dangerous teachings today. It's like blending household chemicals on the stove with your meals. To lend ANY credence to the god of Islam is the same as lending credence to any other false god such as Buddha or L Ron Hubbard (Scientology). Could we blend the daily "horoscope" of the newspaper with Biblical doctrine? No more than we could blend "Roundup", the chemical that kills everything, with "Miracle Grow."

If ANYONE teaches that a saved person can be lost, its false teaching. You are either always saved or you never were. If anyone teaches that a false god such as "Allah" is equal to our God, the God of Abraham , Isaac , and Jacob , our God who sent His Son to die for our sins , then they are false teachers . A while back I asked a good friend and pastor to please let me know if I ever post anything that is contrary to Biblical doctrine.

I want him to hold me accountable. I'm not a pastor or teacher or preacher. I just pass on what God places on my heart, what I've learned, what truths God has revealed through my pastor's teaching through the years. I have several pastors that I contact and ask questions when I'm not sure of something.

When you hear a "suspicious noise" coming from anyone, make sure it's Biblical. Anyone who teaches that Christ's death was in vain because we can lose our salvation is to be carefully scrutinized. Anyone who teaches that Islam or any other false religion or god is just as much god as God, then they are to be disregarded completely. When some "celebrity" such as Oprah Winfrey espouses there being "hundreds of ways" to get to Heaven, there will be many who believe that.

That's the spiritual equivalent of hearing a noise, assuming that it's nothing, and too late realizing that it is someone who has broken in to steal, kill and destroy.

Don't assume that the "noise" you hear is always nothing. Check it out; ask another who is familiar with the Bible. There are many false teachers. Make sure you don't listen to them.

Have a great day everyone.

"But there were also false prophets among the people, even as there will be false teachers among you, who will secretly bring in destructive heresies, even denying the Lord who bought them, and bring on themselves swift destruction. And many will follow their destructive ways, because of whom the way of truth will be blasphemed." 2Peter 2:1-2

Coffee and Prayers

Coffee and Prayers in the Pre-Dawn Hours.

Lots to do today as usual.

I was thinking about a story that someone I know told several years ago.

He had been gone for a couple of weeks to a school, and when he returned home his then-wife was at work.

He walked into the tiny rental house they lived in at the time and he smelled a terrible stench. He walked into the kitchen and there, piled against the back door, were 6 or 7 bags of garbage that had been piled up and never taken out. The smell was terrible, and he began taking the bags to the curb so that the garbage man could pick it up. Ashe carried out the bags, one of the bags broke and he had to stop and pick up the garbage. He was scooping up what he thought was rice at first, and then realized that it wasn't rice that was spilling from the bag. It was moving. It was maggots. The garbage had piled up, began rotting, and had attracted at least one fly, which laid eggs which would have become hundreds of other flies in just a day or so.

Coffee and Prayers

That's the way problems or issues are in life when they aren't dealt with. It piles up and piles up, just like garbage.

Sooner or later, there is a "house full of garbage", so to speak.

When a couple, friends, parents and children, whatever the case may be do not sit down and calmly discuss the issues, then they pile up.

Unlike my example, when it comes to discussion, it takes both or all parties involved to "take out the garbage." One person cannot do it alone. Unfortunately, so many people would just rather not talk about it; they'd rather just gloss over it, just go on with life, and let it pile up. Sooner or later there is no more room for any more, and something has to give. The results can tragically end up with shattered marriages and family, broken relationships, and the end of friendships.

So many people just don't care enough to talk it out. They would rather put all of their anger in their little "anger bank" and withdraw it against the other one whenever they feel like it.
There should always be sitting down, calm discussion, and each person saying "This is how I feel about..." There should never be "You always" or "You never".

Coffee and Prayers

And there should never be name calling, never ever.

There has to be common ground, a common goal, and middle ground that all can agree to.

We also need to "take the garbage out" when it comes to our walk with God. Every day I am in repentance for words, deeds, and actions that I've either done or not done. I see behavior in myself that I don't like and I pray to God for Him to help me conquer this.

Problems within families, marriages, couples, or friends cannot be resolved if they are simply piled up to rot.

God must be at the center of all relationships, and prayer for calm and rational discussion is a must.

When we take out the garbage in our relationships, we never have to worry about that "smell".

We never have to worry about it just sitting there and getting worse by the day. Sooner or later there will be no more room for it.

Get it out. Find common ground.

Coffee and Prayers

Never let a day go by where issues are not resolved.

And when the garbage is taken out, don't bring it back inside. When it's taken out, leave it out. Let it be carried away.

We wouldn't go out to the garbage can and bring in garbage to talk about would we? So why bring up that which has been settled and forgiven?

God doesn't bring up our sins to us when we've confessed. They are as far as the east is from the west. Hebrews 8:12 says: "For I will be merciful to their unrighteousness, and their sins and their lawless deeds I will remember no more."

When it's settled and the trash and garbage is out, leave it out.

Never let a day go by where our sins are not confessed and dealt with.

Have a great day everyone.

"Therefore, putting away lying, 'Let each one of you speak truth with his neighbor, 'for we are members of one another. "Be angry, and do not sin": do not let the sun go down on your wrath, nor give place to the devil. Let him who stole steal no

Coffee and Prayers

longer, but rather let him labor, working with his hands what is good, that he may have something to give him who has need. Let no corrupt word proceed out of your mouth, but what is good for necessary edification, that it may impart grace to the hearers. And do not grieve the Holy Spirit of God, by whom you were sealed for the day of redemption. Let all bitterness, wrath, anger, clamor, and evil speaking be put away from you, with all malice. And be kind to one another, tenderhearted, forgiving one another, even as God in Christ forgave you." Ephesians 4:25-32

Coffee and Prayers this Friday Morning.

We made it through another week. I was thinking this morning of David. What a warrior he was. It's no accident that his star adorns the flag of Israel to this day. I was thinking about how he, at the age of about 14, went out to face a ten foot tall, 500 pound Philistine. A champion that entire armies feared. I was thinking of how he, before facing Goliath, picked up 5 smooth stones. One can visit Israel today and visit the spot and see stones there much like the ones he picked up.

Why do you suppose he picked up 5 stones?

Coffee and Prayers

We know from scripture that Goliath had brothers. David was clearly prepared to kill them all. It only took him one stone to kill this mighty giant. David had no sword, so as this Goliath lay there with a stone buried in his forehead, David took Goliath's own sword and cut off his head. David didn't go out to make peace, he didn't go out to make friends, he didn't go out to try and reason. He went out to destroy this blasphemer and enemy. Are you facing "giants"? Loss of job, loss of family or a loved one?

There are many giants, many enemies that work against us. Also, remember that not all enemies are giants. Some are as hyenas. They prowl around probing for an opening in which they can try and grab a meal they've not earned. Lions don't tolerate hyenas. They will instantly kill them.

The lion knows the hyena cannot be trusted. Ever. People can be hyenas. They sneak and look for openings to try and take what isn't theirs.

Some things, some enemies don't appear gigantic. They may even be unseen. How small is the termite? It's an unseen enemy of a home.

We all need 5 stones when facing our "giants". Think about the situation. Look at it objectively. Suppose you were to advising a friend or loved one on how to handle this. What advice would you give them?

Ready the weapons you have. Do you have spiritual gifts? Insight? Prophesy? A deep understanding of the word? Prepare it. Sharpen it.

Next, TRAIN! As an MP and a soldier in general we TRAIN. We train to take lives, we train to save lives. We train to accomplish the mission.

Train yourself for what you are facing. David had trained all his life. Yes he was just a shepherd boy, but all his life he had protected his flock. He had killed the lion and the bear that came against him and his flock. Train by being in the word, praying, getting the needed skills to do this.

Next, move TOWARDS your giant.

David RAN TOWARD his giant. He didn't hesitate, he didn't back down. He ran towards him and struck the first blow. The death blow. He didn't mess around.

Finally, cut off the head. Nothing can survive without a head.

These 5 stones will help you in no matter what you face.

Coffee and Prayers

Don't let a small matter grow into a giant. If it's something small, it will keep growing. It may seem harmless; it may seem okay now, but picture the future of what it may grow into. Is it worth it? Kill it now.

A habit, a relationship with someone who is causing trouble. Spending habits. Think about this. Goliath was once a little baby. He grew into a giant.

Baby hyenas grow into adult hyenas. Tiny snakes grow into big snakes.

If you can kill it in its infancy, do it. If it's already a giant, kill it.

Have a great day everyone.

"So it was, when the Philistine arose and came and drew near to meet David, that David hurried and ran toward the army to meet the Philistine. Then David put his hand in his bag and took out a stone; and he slung it and struck the

Philistine in his forehead, so that the stone sank into his forehead, and he fell on his face to the earth. So David prevailed over the Philistine with a sling and a stone, and struck the Philistine and killed him. But there was no sword in the hand of David. Therefore David ran and stood over the

Philistine, took his sword and drew it out of its sheath and killed him, and cut off his head with it. And when the Philistines saw that their champion was dead, they fled." 1Samuel 17:48-51

Coffee and Prayers this Freezing Cold Morning.

I was so pleased that Cindy got up and knelt beside the bed with me and we prayed together this morning. We pray together at meal time, but prayers together morning and night are needed as well. I pray much alone, but need to lead my family in family prayer more. This is something I vow to work to improve.

I was glad to see so many positive posts about a great Christmas. I love seeing pics of great times like that and reading about them.

So now, Christmas is over. Trash bags are full of torn wrapping paper and boxes. Soon of not already, decorations will come down, ornaments will be put away; the tree will be taken down. All of the visual reminders of Christmas will be put in storage for another year.

Coffee and Prayers

A new year will be here, school will start back, and life will get back to "normal."

So how do we maintain the joy of Christmas? I don't mean being "happy." I mean JOY.

I've heard of people who will say "I'm always happy." People who say that they "refuse" to let themselves be unhappy , refuse to let themselves be upset , or to have any "negative emotions."

That's sort of like saying that you refuse to let yourself get hungry or thirsty or tired. If you have a life, emotions are a natural part of it. If you see someone who has only one emotion ("happy") every hour of every day, then likely they are like a pressure cooker that is on the stove and no steam is escaping. It's all inside and will blow up at some point.

Emotions are natural, and life will bring out the sad, the angry, the frustrating, the happy, all of our natural emotions.

There is nothing wrong with that. There were times when even Jesus felt down. There were times when even He got angry. Jesus wept, He felt sorrow, He felt deeply troubled, and He felt anger. One only needs to read the Gospels to see this.

Coffee and Prayers

Jesus even asked His 12 disciples (John 6:67) "Do you also want to go away?" when many of His other disciples left Him. He didn't cover up or hide His emotions.

So how do we, after a season of joy, maintain that joy? Yes, life will bring us sorrow and sadness, anger, hurt, and so on. And there is nothing wrong with emotions. God MADE us emotional beings. The thing is to not let sadness; hurt, anger and all RULE our lives. We can be angry and not sin (Eph 4:26). Being sad, upset, and so on isn't bad unless it totally rules us. If Jesus showed all these emotions, then why do we feel that we should always put on our best face for the public and never show any other side of ourselves? We have to remember that happiness depends upon a "happening". We can't be "happy" all of the time, but we CAN have JOY all of the time.

We can have the joy of Christmas 365 days a year when we have the joy of CHRIST. Yes we will run the gamut of emotions that life brings. We will feel sad, blue, angry, lonely, and so on, but even that cannot steal our JOY.

There will be times when we feel like it is us against the world. There will be ups and downs. We will go through valleys, because life just hurts sometimes. We have to maintain out joy however. We can be crying our eyes out over hurt and pain, but yet feel joy, if we keep the joy of His salvation. Even when alone, we are not alone. We know that He is with us. Even when we weep and mourn and feel such emptiness, He is there to comfort us.

Even in days of sorrow, we must keep out joy and we can when we keep Him as the center of our lives. When the joy of a season has passed, we can keep our joy of life, all of our lives.

Have a great day everyone.

"Then he said to them, 'Go your way, eat the fat, drink the sweet, and send portions to those for whom nothing is prepared; for this day is holy to our Lord. Do not sorrow, for the joy of the Lord is your strength.'" Nehemiah 8:10

Coffee and Prayers this Friday Morning.

A long day today, but the weekend begins afterwards .I wanted to repost something from well over a year ago. I hope that it will help someone today. I was thinking about a movie that came out during the early 90's titled "Regarding Henry." It starred Harrison Ford as Henry Turner, a high powered New York attorney. Henry was ruthless, aggressive, heartless, and unethical. He brought in millions to the firm in which he worked. His wife Sarah (Annette Benning) was a socialite, and his 11 year-old daughter Rachel feared him.

His most recent victory had been defending a multimillion dollar lawsuit against a hospital whose mistake had caused the permanent disablement of a man. Henry had hidden a witness statement that would have proven the hospital negligent.

As Henry stopped in a store to buy a pack of cigarettes, he interrupted a robbery. He was shot in the head and chest. Although nearly killed, he did survive. He suffered brain damage and loss of memory. As he learned to walk and talk again, he now had an almost childlike personality. He had a childlike fascination with the huge Manhattan penthouse he lived in with his family, decorated by his wife and paid for by his extravagant fees. He had barely even noticed anyone or anything but himself before. His daughter and he were now becoming very close. He now laughed at spilled drinks instead of punishing her for it. Rachel even taught him to read again.

Now his wife Sarah discovered that she was falling in love with him again, while before she was having an affair, as was Henry. Her socialite "friends" now laughed behind her back, joking that she now had

Coffee and Prayers

"two children." The law firm that he had built now let him come back just to do "busy work", but not to practice law.

Henry, Sarah, and Rachel are now happier than they have ever been, despite a loss of income and social status.

The movie has a great twist in the end as well.

I say all that to say this. There are so many of us who were "Henry" before Christ saved us, changed us. There are so many murderers, killers, gangsters, thieves , adulterers, on and on and on, who received a "bullet " to the heart and head from Christ who are now completely different people than they were . Life is so like that when we are saved. We speak softer (for the most part). We appreciate the small things, we love deeper, we are kinder, we are gentler, and we have a child like faith.

And yes, there are going to be those who laugh behind our backs at us. Just as Henry and Sarah were in this movie. God can use many ways and circumstances to change our hearts. It won't take a gunshot to the head or chest .Most times it's just that still, soft voice. I've heard testimony of drug addicts who just suddenly were called by God and just immediately put away their drugs and became new. I've heard testimonies from people who were in a bar, heard His voice, and was immediately changed, put down their drink and never touched one again. I've heard, in person, the testimony of Michael Franzese, a former captain of the Colombo crime family. It was Christ who changed him from a man who could strike fear with just a glance into a new man. I could list dozens more.

God uses many ways to change us. And once we are changed, there is no going back. People can laugh at the "new" you. They can marvel at how "successful" the old you was when you were ruthless, heartless, and would stop at nothing to get what you wanted. They can make fun of you all they want. They can kick you off the "social ladder", which you won't want nor care about anyway. They can do all of this, but with Christ as your Savior, they cannot steal the joy that is yours. They can never change you back into what you once were. Has He changed you? He sure has me and He is working on me every day. Have a great day everyone.

"Therefore, if anyone is in Christ, he is a new creation; old things have passed away; behold, all things have become new." 2 Corinthians 5:17

Coffee and Prayers

Coffee and Prayers this Tuesday Morning.

Much to do today, as I'll be headed out for Annual Training this week.

I was thinking about one of my all-time favorite movies, "Con Air". In the movie, Army Ranger Cameron Poe (Nicholas Cage) has finished his time in service and has returned to his wife, newly pregnant wife, Tricia in Mobile. A gang of 3 men attack them in the parking lot of the small bar where Tricia works; Poe defends his wife and himself, killing one attacker with his bare hands. Poe is then sentenced to 8 years in a maximum security prison. He makes only one friend during his incarceration, his name is "Baby-O". He is serving in a prison in California, and when he is granted parole and going home, they send him and Baby-O aboard the US Marshal's plane. On board are the absolute worse of the worse criminals, the mastermind of them, Cyrus Grissam, has devised a plan along with others to take over the plane. Now Baby-O was diabetic and was to receive his insulin in flight. When the criminals take over, Baby-O's syringe is crushed, and now the guards, including a woman guard named Sally Bishop, are all prisoners of the criminals, including the most notorious serial rapist, "Johnny 23". Bishop is defended by Poe, who saved her from him.

Coffee and Prayers

And then during a chance to get off the plane , Poe refuses, he stays on to try to save Baby-O, who is without his insulin and getting sick, and he won't leave Bishop at the mercy of a rapist . Baby-O tells Poe "There you are trying to be a Ranger! You're not a Ranger anymore, you're a convict!"

Being in prison didn't change what Poe was. His circumstances didn't change who he was. What even his friend said about him didn't change who and what Poe was. An Army Ranger. And of course Poe goes on to save the day.

So what of us who are Christians? Have we ever been in a situation, be it of our own making or not and had someone say of us "He's not really a Christian." "She's not a

Christian." After all, how can you be a Christian and be divorced? How can you be a Christian and your teen daughter is pregnant? How can you be a Christian and your son is on drugs? How can you be a Christian and have financial problems? On and on and on. People will label us .They see something bad in our life and they say "Aha! God's punishing them!" They are so quick to point a finger .They are so quick to say "I'm a success, they are a failure, I'm a better Christian." They may not even be a Christian and say "Where is your God?" In that movie, Poe was in a situation, and even his friend disputed who he was due to his circumstances.

Look at so many people of the Bible. Did circumstances and location determine who they were? Suppose we could say "Look at that Joseph! Some man of God! He's a slave, now he's in prison, accused of rape." So would that change who Joseph was? Moses was a Prince of Egypt. Then he was out in the wilderness, having nothing in the world. A man of God? Then he wasn't even allowed into the land of promise.

Look at Paul, thrown into prison many times.

And what about even Christ? Many doubted who HE was. There He was, executed in the most painful and humiliating way ever devised by man. Tried and found guilty and crucified between two thieves.

Did even those circumstances change who He was and still is? Not at all.

The enemy will use any method, any circumstance, anybody to try to tell you that you're not the person you know you are, the person God made you. You're a child of the King regardless of your circumstances. Just like Poe was in prison, convicted of manslaughter, he was still a Ranger.

Coffee and Prayers

That never changed. You will never change. When HE changes you, you're changed forever.

Have a great day everyone.

"Therefore, if anyone is in Christ, he is a new creation; old things have passed away; behold, all things have become new." 2 Corinthians 5:17

Coffee and Prayers this Cold Monday Morning.

I wanted to repost this from a year ago.

Yesterday I was thinking about how several years ago I and some others were talking about carrying a gun. A woman in the conversation told me that if I carried a gun, kept a gun at home, then it showed no faith in God's protection.

She said that she had faith that He would protect her, her husband and family.

I asked her if she had health insurance, homeowners insurance, and car insurance.
She replied "Of course". When I asked why, she replied that it was in case they got sick or got into an accident.

Coffee and Prayers

I then said "So you don't depend on God's protection for these areas?" She said that I was comparing apples to oranges. I told her that I simply couldn't understand saying that you trust God to protect you for one thing, but not something else. You either totally trust God to never allow anything bad to happen to you, or you don't. Why would you trust God to protect you from a criminal, but not from an accident, cancer, and so on?

Yes, we have to have faith, but God also gives us sense to take certain measures.
He told Moses to have all the children of Israel to put the blood of the lamb on their doorpost to save them from death. They had to take action.

God has instructed people throughout the Bible to take certain actions for protection, including wiping out other tribes, just as He instructed Israel to do.

How do we determine what is "blind faith", and what is faith in action?

As I said, God gives us the sense to take certain protective measures for ourselves and our families. Yes, we trust God to protect us ultimately, but do we drive without insurance? Do we go without health insurance because we trust Him to always keep us healthy? God has NEVER promised that we

Coffee and Prayers

will never have an accident or other things in life. Yes we are to have faith, but we have to have works as well. If the flood waters are rising all about you, do you get out of your house and go to higher ground, or do you sit in your house and trust Him to save you from drowning? James 2:14-17 tells us that faith without works is dead.

Yes we are to have faith, but we are to also take steps to protect ourselves. We must take actions. A farmer prays for a good crop, but he must till the land, plant his seeds, fertilize, cultivate, and harvest. He doesn't sit back in his chair and expect it to just come to him. God blesses him through his faith and his works.

Pray with expectation and faith, and take the action needed to protect you. Again I say, we are not promised a life of no troubles and all. But we are promised that He is there with us. Have a great day everyone.

Consider the words of Christ Jesus.

"'These things I have spoken to you, that in Me you may have peace. In the world you will have tribulation; but be of good cheer, I have overcome the world.'" John 16:33

Coffee and Prayers this Friday Morning.

Many years ago, my grandmother and I were walking through her pasture, and I noticed her pulling some plants up. A yellow flower like plant. When I asked her about it, she said that it was bitter weed. She explained that if the cows ate it, it would make their milk bitter.

I remember thinking about what a pretty little yellow flower that it had. But yet, it would make the milk bitter, as well as butter that was made from the milk. And if a newborn calf couldn't nurse because of the bitterness, it could die.

That story brought to mind a small bag of apples that I bought last week. As I grabbed one out of the bag, I noticed that several had bad spots on them. Especially the ones that were around one especially bad one. It reminded me of the saying "One bad apple spoils the whole barrel." It's true that a bad or spoiled apple can ruin those around it. And those in turn eventually ruin all.

Do you remember how in school it seemed as if there was always one or two who were always disrupting class, getting in trouble, or getting others into trouble?

Coffee and Prayers

There are many ways that bad company can corrupt good people. I've heard of and have witnessed all of my life, people who were brought to trouble by hanging out with the "wrong crowd".

There is always going to be that one person who is going to keep trouble stirred up. That one person who is going to be at the center of strife and controversy. Some people live for it.

The Bible warns us how we can be ensnared by keeping such company. In 1 Corinthians 15:33 we read: Do not be deceived: "Evil company corrupts good habits."

We also see that in Proverbs 13:20 that Solomon warns "He who walks with wise men will be wise, but the companion of fools will be destroyed." In Proverbs 14:7 he writes "Go from the presence of a foolish man, When you do not perceive in him the lips of knowledge." And also he warns how bad company can corrupt in Proverbs 25:26 "A righteous man who falters before the wicked is like a murky spring and a polluted well."

We also learn how those can get our very souls ensnared. Proverbs 22:24-25
"Make no friendship with an angry man, and with a furious man do not go, lest you learn his ways and set a snare for your soul."

Coffee and Prayers

In Psalm 26:5 David writes "I have hated the assembly of evildoers, and will not sit with the wicked."

The Psalmist also warns of similar in Psalm 199:115 "Depart from me, you evildoers, for I will keep the commandments of my God!"

Yes, Jesus ate with sinners. But they changed their ways and followed Him, or He disassociated with them. In Matthew 10 He instructed this of His disciples:

"And when you go into a household, greet it. If the household is worthy, let your peace come upon it. But if it is not worthy, let your peace return to you. And whoever will not receive you nor hear your words, when you depart from that house or city, shake off the dust from your feet.

Assuredly, I say to you, it will be more tolerable for the land of Sodom and Gomorrah in the Day of Judgment than for that city!"

We can only do so much. If some will not heed the truth from the very mouth of Jesus, we certainly can't expect everyone to heed our words of salvation either. Paul and Barnabus put this into action in Acts 13:51 when they were rejected.

Coffee and Prayers

Letting some people close is much like the pretty bitterweed. It may look harmless, but can lead to death.

Remember that some aren't going to change. Ever. And that they will only corrupt those around. Have a great day everyone.

"Blessed is the man who walks not in the counsel of the ungodly, Nor stands in the path of sinners, Nor sits in the seat of the scornful; But his delight is in the law of the Lord, And in His law he meditates day and night. He shall be like a tree Planted by the rivers of water, That brings forth its fruit in its season, Whose leaf also shall not wither; And whatever he does shall prosper." Psalm 1:1-3

Coffee and Prayers this Cool Friday Morning.

Looking forward to seeing my new bride today. It seems that nearly every day on the news I hear of the American flag being banned. Not overseas, here in the USA. Why? Even here in the USA, children have been sent home from school for wearing American flag shirts.

Coffee and Prayers

Some don't want you to show your patriotism. Some may be "offended" is the argument. Really? There's not a day that goes by that I am free from seeing grown men with their pants down, underwear showing, and this offends a lot of people, yet it's "protected speech."

And what about publicly proclaiming your faith, your love of Christ? Some don't want you telling it in public. They don't want you reading your Bible at work or school. They don't want you to wear your cross. They don't want to see your verses framed on your desk or on your wall. They don't want to read your posts on Facebook if you post about your faith. They'd much rather you keep it to yourself.

Don't display your menorah, your Star of David. Don't display your manger scene or cross.
Even some in church with you may not want to see you standing up, hands raised in worship. They feel they know better how "worship", as they would call it, can be done than the Holy Spirit does.

They roll their eyes at those who post prayer requests, praise reports and so on.

They'd much rather read of your love of a sports team than of our Savior. They would rather see where you checked in for dinner than anything else. They say you "wear your religion on your

Coffee and Prayers

sleeve". Well I don't have a religion, I have a relationship. And yes I wear it on my sleeve; I don't keep it hidden in the closet.

I've prayed as to whether or not to post my morning posts and God gave me this verse; Matthew 10:27 "Whatever I tell you in the dark, speak in the light; and what you hear in the ear, preach on the housetops."

That's my answer.

They say they support your right to speak about God and your other beliefs, they just wish you'd shut up about it.

It's not new, not just in this day. People are going to hate you for your faith. The early disciples lost their lives for proclaiming Him.

Now we see hostility against Him everywhere.

If we don't live up to someone's standards, they feel we aren't "qualified" to speak of redemption, forgiveness, blessings, healing, restoration, rebirth, and grace. Who are WE, these miserable hypocrites and sinners to speak of salvation through His death and resurrection?

Coffee and Prayers

Every day or two I try to check myself that I'm not saying "God is on my side", but that I am on God's side.

No, I'm not saying that it's wrong if you don't proclaim your faith or speak of your relationship with Him. That's not for me or anyone else to speak of. I just know that I am not ashamed of my relationship with Him. I AM ashamed that my words and actions don't always reflect this. He convicts my heart of it, and His grace covers it. As I heard a preacher named Mickey Bonner say many years ago, "When you're saved, you can't get away with anything!" And there isn't a day He isn't convicting my heart and hearing my prayer of repentance.

We will be hated, reviled, laughed at, and gossiped about. We are in good company. Consider the words of Christ, and have a great day. Stay warm today.

"'Blessed are you when they revile and persecute you, and say all kinds of evil against you falsely for My sake. Rejoice and be exceedingly glad, for great is your reward in heaven, for so they persecuted the prophets who were before you. "You are the salt of the earth; but if the salt loses its flavor, how shall it be seasoned? It is then good for nothing but to be thrown out and trampled underfoot by men.

Coffee and Prayers

'You are the light of the world. A city that is set on a hill cannot be hidden. Nor do they light a lamp and put it under a basket, but on a lampstand, and it gives light to all who are in the house. Let your light so shine before men, that they may see your good works and glorify your Father in heaven.'" Matthew 5:11-16

Coffee and Prayers this Saturday Morning.

Thursday afternoon, I noticed the brick fence around a yard at a house about a half a mile from our house.

The entire east side of the fence had fallen. This was a nice looking red brick fence. I wondered if the homeowner was going to fix it. I wondered about the cost of fixing it.

Then I thought about why it fell. Without even stopping to examine it, I knew that the reason that it fell was that the foundation was weak. Or maybe it had no foundation at all. I knew that the massive amount of rain had made the ground very soft, and that combined with the wind caused it to collapse.

This fence had likely survived many storms over the years. It had seen much, yet it finally fell.

Coffee and Prayers

Life can be like that. We can survive much, and then we collapse. Or we never collapse.

What makes the difference? The foundation. There are many brick fences in the area. Not all of them collapsed. That's because not all of them were built alike.

Why is it that some people can stand strong in the face of storms when others collapse?
A change in a financial situation can cause some people to collapse. When the market crashed in 1929, many people who lived only for the value of the stock they owned and the wealth generated by it committed suicide.

Money was their foundation.

Many people will collapse after a divorce or death in the family. And some people will collapse when their health changes.

Why? They have no foundation.

Why is it that some can face financial upheavals, changes in relationships, and health setbacks with full faith and confidence? It's because of their foundation.

Coffee and Prayers

I think of Job, who lost his wealth, his children, and then his health. He was a man of prominence, then there he was sitting on the ground, scraping the many sores on his body with broken pottery. His friends were telling him that he really must have messed up for God to be punishing him like that, and on top of all, his wife was telling him that he should just "curse God and die."

Job answered all of this, to sum it up, with this in Job 13:15, "Though He slay me, yet will I trust Him."

Where is your foundation? Is your foundation your job? Your savings? Your retirement? Your health? Your relationships? All of those things that can leave, become worthless, be taken, change, are they what you lean on?

The Lord isn't going to leave you if you're His. He isn't going to forsake you if you're His.
Have a great day everyone.

"'Therefore whoever hears these sayings of Mine, and does them, I will liken him to a wise man who built his house on the rock: and the rain descended, the floods came, and the winds blew and beat on that house; and it did not fall, for it was founded on the rock. "But everyone who hears these sayings of mine, and does not do them, will be like a foolish man who built his house on the sand: and the rain descended, the floods came, and the winds blew and beat on that house; and it fell. And great was its fall.'" Matthew 7:24-27

Coffee and Prayers this Cold Monday Morning.

Headed in for a 12 hour tour.

I caught the end of a news story the other day. I didn't hear all of it, but there was a woman who was suing her employer because they would not refer to her as "gender neutral." She was a woman, but wanted to be referred to as "gender neutral." Now there are some things that you cannot be "neutral" in. Gender is one. Yes I know there are eunuchs in the Bible, but I'm referring to us all, today. You are born male or female. There is no neutrality. It's one or the other.

So many people just want to remain "neutral" about everything. They don't vote, they want to be "neutral". But they don't realize that by NOT voting, it's giving one candidate a vote. They see a robbery, or someone being assaulted .They walk away. They don't want to get involved. Their being "neutral" gives the bad guy a victory.

They see a wrong and they stay "neutral". They don't want to be involved.

Now yes there are some things that being neutral WON'T matter in. Now I love sports, but if I'm watching a game on TV and don't really care which team wins, then I've made no difference. Even if I'm extremely passionate about one team, I still am no factor in the outcome.

There are things that being "neutral" about will never matter in this world.

People who are "neutral" about the things that matter are like a car that is in neutral. They can be pushed anywhere. They can roll unguided.

So what about being "neutral" about the Lord? Can you be? No you can't.

It's like what Bryan said in his sermon yesterday. "When Jesus is brought into the conversation, it changes everything." He is either hated, feared, or loved.

Jesus, the cross ... You can't be neutral. Why is it that the name of Jesus changes everything?

Coffee and Prayers

Because HE changed everything! Why is it that He is either loved, feared or hated? Because He is God. He is the Messiah. Across, the symbol of our salvation, stirs us in some way. We hear the name Jesus and it stirs us in some way. We see a painting or picture representing Him and it stirs us in some way.

Are you for Him? Do you know Him? Do you CLAIM to be neutral? He said (Matthew 12:30) "He who is not with Me is against Me, and he who does not gather with Me scatters abroad."

You can decide that you are going to be neutral in life. You can decide that you will never take a stand for or against anything.

You may think that your life is safe inside your "bubble" of neutrality, but your neutrality affects others and you.

You can't look at Him, at the cross, and be neutral. Are you His? You either are or not. There is no neutral in salvation. Have a great day everyone.

"'I know your works, that you are neither cold nor hot. I could wish you were cold or hot. So then, because you are lukewarm, and neither cold nor hot, I will vomit you out of My mouth. Because you say, 'I am rich, have become wealthy, and have need of nothing'—and do not know that you are wretched, miserable, poor, blind, and naked—'" Rev 3:15-17

Coffee and Prayers this Cold, Foggy Morning.

This past week I heard a story about an 18 year old young lady in New Jersey who is suing her parents. This girl is an honor student, but refused to do as she was told, so she ended up leaving home. She then sued her parents for support! This girl feels that she is entitled to that which her parents earned. She feels that she has a right to have bills, tuition, and so on paid by her parents.

Now, if her parents just wanted to, they could support her the rest of her life. They, however, other than food, clothing, and shelter, are not REQUIRED to provide anything other than love and care for their child. Monetary support is an option for the parents.

Does she feel that since she was an "honors student", she is entitled? Perhaps. Does she feel that her grades alone has entitled her? Sounds like it.

Coffee and Prayers

So what about us in our relationship, or lack of relationship with God? Aren't some that way with God? They feel that since they are "good", they are entitled. They feel that since they are "successful ", they are entitled. Entitled to His kingdom. They feel that since they did this and that, they are heaven bound one day. Since they throw God's name out there now and then, they are entitled. But some don't truly even have any relationship with Him. They never pray, they never read His word, they never even consider Him.

They may have HEAD knowledge of Him, but they have no HEART knowledge of Him. It's sorta like their relationship with a Governor or something. Yes, they know he exists, but they don't know him, never spoke to him. Wouldn't recognize his voice if He spoke to them. Some feel that maybe because they are wealthy, God favors them. Or maybe God has nothing to do with it at all. I've heard millionaires such as Ted Turner say similar.

However, Jesus Himself said that He causes the sun to rise on the evil and the good, and the rain to fall on the just and the unjust. (Matt 5:45) In other words, He waters the crops of the unjust along with just.

So what entitles us to His kingdom? Can we make a list of all that we have done? Can we list all that we haven't done? What all reasons can we give? If we were to "sue" God for our share of His kingdom, what can we use to make our case?

Can we list our education? Our grades? Our career? Our savings? Our 401K? Our home? Our car? Could I show Him any certificate or diploma from any school or training I've attended? Will my military service count? No. What did the thief on the cross have to offer or show?

The one and ONLY thing I have is that I am His, I belong to Jesus. That's all that counts, it's all I need. When the thief on the cross said to Him "Remember me", He said "Today you will be with me in paradise." He didn't ask him to show any good, he didn't ask for any credentials or pedigrees. Will we stand at the gates and have to make our case for entry? Or will He already know us? There is nothing that I can do to earn my entry to His kingdom. There are no works I can show. It's not about whom we are, it's about what HE'S done. It's not about what we've done; it's about who HE IS.

We don't earn it, He gives it freely. All we have to do is accept it. We can't improve on it, we can't change it.

We are saved through grace. His amazing grace.

Coffee and Prayers

We can't sue for it. We can't petition for it. We can't earn it, we can't buy it, we can't list any reason we "deserve" it.

I'm just a sinner, saved by grace. All of us who are saved are. Are you His? I sure hope so. Have a great day everyone.

"For by grace you have been saved through faith, and that not of yourselves; it is the gift of God, not of works, lest anyone should boast. For we are His workmanship, created in Christ Jesus for good works, which God prepared beforehand that we should walk in them." Ephesians 2:8-10

"You lust and do not have. You murder and covet and cannot obtain. You fight and war. Yet you do not have because you do not ask. You ask and do not receive, because you ask amiss, that you may spend it on your pleasures." James 4:2-3

Coffee and Prayers this Morning.

I posted this several times before, but it is heavy on my mind again. When an incident hasn't occurred in a while, we tend to become complacent.

Coffee and Prayers

There was a church shooting yesterday, so I want to post this that posted a couple of years ago. The case for armed security in our churches:

I've been working on this for several weeks. The events of this week have made me put it to print.

This may be long, but I hope it convinces most, especially after this week what churches need to do.

Having experience in this matter in the military and police, and serving in the past on security details at church (we carry concealed) qualifies me to speak of this.

Why church security? I've heard people laugh and scoff and say they'd never attend a church where there "had" to be security. They say it shows no faith. Well, by that logic, so does having insurance on your home, car and health.

Let's address this issue. First of all, you have to realize that church isn't a sacred place to everyone. Most people believe, wrongly, that no one would do anything bad at a church, because after all, it's CHURCH. We will address this.

There are four elements, or scenarios, that are cases for armed security.

Coffee and Prayers

The first element is the criminal element. The normal person sees a church service and only sees faithful people worshipping. A criminal or criminals do not see this. They see a soft target. Maybe a petty theft, just wandering around the parking lot, looking for purses on car seats. A carelessly unlocked car door or two. Maybe break out a window and make off with some cash and credit cards.

Maybe they think a little bigger. At church there is cash for tithes and offerings. There are dozens of helpless people, all in a building, ripe for the picking. An armed robbery perhaps.

The second element is the domestic element.

Imagine a divorce. A violent man has been prohibited from seeing his child or children.

He knows the mother puts them in kid's church, or they are in the youth section. He's decided that he's not going to let anyone keep him from seeing his kids. He knows they are going to be in church, no one to stop him except the little lady who leads kid's church, or some young youth pastor.

The third element is the mentally insane element. I had another scenario in mind, but the church shooting in Texas yesterday is a good scenario.

Coffee and Prayers

Someone who hates religions, Christianity in particular, what better place to go kill a few Christians than a church?

Some people may just hate what the pastor preaches.

There are also many more people who would love to kill a pastor and as many believers as possible just because of what they believe.

There is also the fourth element. The terror element. We are at war with Islam. What better place to strike fear than by striking a church? A small town church with limited first responders, a building full of unarmed people, all attacked to cause fear. This is especially true for our Jewish brethren.

You see, I've been trained to think like a criminal thinks, to think how a terrorist would think. To think how the enemy thinks.

Church is NOT SACRED to any of the elements I've listed. To think that church is "safe" is as naive a notion as thinking that all criminals, insane persons, and terrorists hold the same values that we have.

Coffee and Prayers

So. Here is how we conducted and trained security in a church.

We had an outer ring of security that patrols the parking lot. Preventing an incident is the best way to go. Stopping any incident in the parking lot.

There is also a middle ring of security. The lobby, hallways, entrances are covered. There is also an inner ring of security. Strategic locations inside the sanctuary are manned. All areas are watched.

Each person on duty has his weapon concealed, and has a radio and earpiece. Communication is vital.

We ran "active shooter drills" after church. We went through scenarios.

We, on duty, had to learn that we had to put worship aside for that time. What did we look for?

If it was a warm day and I saw someone wearing a coat, I'd watch him. If I saw someone who was unfamiliar, looking around, I watched him. If I saw someone walk in who just looked as if he (or she) just wasn't there for church, they garnered my attention, as well as the others on duty.

Coffee and Prayers

Outer security may call on the radio and say there were several people casing the parking lot. Someone would respond as back up to outer security.

Some will say that they would never stand for security at "their" church.

Well, these are the times that we live in. But in fact, if you read 1 Chronicles 26, you will read that there was "security" duties assigned for the early Temple in David's time.

We cannot think that church is sacred to those who don't even consider life sacred. Church is no more sacred to the above elements than a Dollar General Store is.

Church isn't safe. And having security in church doesn't show a "lack of faith" any more than having insurance is a lack of faith. Or wearing a seatbelt.

Take a minute to consider how an enemy thinks to destroy what we consider sacred, rather than to think that an enemy considers sacred the things we consider sacred.

Consider lastly the words of Jesus.

Coffee and Prayers

"Then He said to them, 'But now, he who has a money bag, let him take it, and likewise a knapsack; and he who has no sword, let him sell his garment and buy one.'" Luke 22:36

Coffee and Prayers this Cold Tuesday Morning.

I was thinking about a few years ago a co-worker of mine had bought a pistol and asked me if I could clean it for him and tell me what I thought of it. I of course told him I would.

When I got home and looked at it, I could see the problems right away. The brand name was "Bryco" I think. I'd never heard of the brand. I'm familiar with quality name brand weapons. Kimber, Smith & Wesson, Glock, Sig, Colt, and so on.

But the problems with this pistol were so obvious to me. First of all, it felt like a brick in my hand. There were no sights, only a sight "channel", a groove down the length of the barrel. There was no slide lock. No way to lock the slide to the rear. And the magazine release? You had to turn the pistol (I can't bring myself to say weapon on this one, as it didn't meet my requirements) upside down and with one hand pull the magazine release, which was on the bottom of the magazine well, and with the other hand pull the magazine out.

This was a terribly designed pistol. My friend Terry had bought this as a defense to protect his family. I gave him my honest assessment of it. I told him that it was no good. When he declared that he had paid $125 for it, I told him he paid $100 too much for it. I told him that he needed to spend the money and get a quality weapon that he could rely on to protect his family and I told him the features that a good quality weapon has, and the name brands that he should choose from. I told him that people buy these because they are cheap, often used in crimes, and then tossed away.

Now when I sat down to write this, I had something totally different as my main point.

I began to think of worth. What is our worth as human beings? I see homeless people whom others see as "worthless." I see those who are in addiction whom others see as "worthless." I see single moms whom some see as "worthless." I see troubled teens, broken families, people who have experienced bankruptcy, loss of jobs, and so on whom some call "worthless." Me and my best friend Robbie were talking the other day about how some people do not want to be around anyone who doesn't have what they have or more. If they are not in some way to be of use to them, then they are of no use. If they can't provide something to them at some point, then they aren't worth their time.

And every one of us are that way to Satan. He hates us more than we could ever imagine. We are worth less than zero. He will use us, no doubt, and we are of use to him, but are worthless to him. He will, as a crook would do with a cheap pistol, use people to commit his crimes, his sins, anything that is against God.

Jesus was crucified between two thieves. He was viewed as worthless. He was viewed as weak, a trouble maker. One who spoke out against the pious, the "religious", and the ones who set the rules.

To them, they saw victory as He hung on the cross. Naked, beaten, bloody, suffering the worst pain and humiliation and shame imaginable.

And our worth to HIM? He loves us so much He suffered that for us. People will treat us as a criminal treats a cheap pistol. Satan certainly will as well. We all have more flaws than a cheap pistol, but He loves us as though we are perfect. When we

Coffee and Prayers

are His, it doesn't matter what we lack. He makes us perfect through Him.

Don't let people declare your worth. They can't.

He loves you so much He died for you. He died for us, so we may live for Him. Even one of those worthless thieves who died next to Him wears a crown now, as he experienced salvation on the cross.

Don't look at your bank account, your home, your car, your job for your "worth." Look at the cross for your worth.

Have a great day everyone.

"'Whatever I tell you in the dark, speak in the light; and what you hear in the ear, preach on the housetops. And do not fear those who kill the body but cannot kill the soul. But rather fear Him who is able to destroy both soul and body in hell. Are not two sparrows sold for a copper coin? And not one of them falls to the ground apart from your Father's will. But the very hairs of your head are all numbered. Do not fear therefore; you are of more value than many sparrows.

"Therefore whoever confesses Me before men, him I will also confess before My Father who is in

Coffee and Prayers

Heaven. But whoever denies Me before men, him I will also deny before My Father who is in heaven.'" Matthew 10:27-33

Coffee and Prayers this Thursday Morning.

I was thinking about the last time I was on my parent's hill pond fishing. As I was hoping to hit the lake or a hill pond to fish here real soon, I was thinking about what entices fish to bite. I love to bass fish to catch and release, but crappie fish to catch and eat. The water was so calm the last time; I was thinking how my "broken minnow" (a minnow lure hinged in the middle, the front floats, the rear sinks) would be great. To cast it towards fish cover and watch a bass hit it as soon as it hits the water is a thrill. I have so many different lures in my tackle box, as do most people who fish; there is an endless supply of something to entice a fish to bite. Spinner baits, crank baits, deep runners, top water, jigs, and so on.

The idea is to use something enticing.

It made me think about what Satan has in his tackle box to entice us into biting into sin, reeling us in, and destroying us. His very first and successful lure to mankind was a piece of fruit. But he has a tackle box full of deadly lures. Money, power, glory, highs, sex, riches, fame, and so on.

How many times has he dangled that lure of fast money to people who have gambling addictions, only for them to realize, too late, that they are hooked and lose all?

How many times has he dangled a "high" to people, then then each subsequent "high" takes more and more of the substance to achieve that high, hooking them in addiction?

How many times has he dangled a pretty face and a short skirt, or a handsome face to hook a man or woman, then adultery has destroyed their lives or family?

How many times has he dangled the lure of "no more pain" and caused someone to end their life? Every time that you read or hear of some tragedy, it's because Satan has lured someone in with a lie. A lie meant to destroy them. Jesus made His disciples "fishers of men " to SAVE THEM, to save all who believe in Him, follow Him, trust Him, belong to Him. Satan loves it when a person is addicted to something destructive. He loves it when families and marriages and relationships and finances are destroyed. He loves to hook people, reel them in, place his thumb in their mouth and smile as they are hopeless, about to be eaten or mounted on his wall. Jesus can free us. He can get the hook out no matter how deep it's swallowed. He and He alone can set us free.

Don't follow that lure of Satan. Its end is a means of death. Only Christ can get us off of that hook and set us free.

Have a great day everyone.

"'The thief does not come except to steal, and to kill, and to destroy. I have come that they may have life, and that they may have it more abundantly.'" John 10:10

Coffee and Prayers this Cold Thursday.

The weekend is in sight.

I was watching a video of Israeli PM Benjamin Netanyahu the other day. He was speaking about how the countries that wish to destroy Israel shall fail.

From the time God formed the nation and people of Israel, her enemies have sought to destroy her.

Coffee and Prayers

To no avail. Indecent history, in 1948 when Israel was recognized by the United Nations and was attacked by 8 hostile Arab countries and they all were soundly defeated. As have all nations who have attacked her since. Many Israeli Army veterans have said that there were mysterious soldiers who just "appeared" on the battlefield fighting side by side with the Israelis. Angels, sent by God.

The USA was the First Nation to recognize Israel when they became a "recognized" nation in 1948. The years after this saw a tremendous blessing to our country until the times we went against Israel.

Any time that the USA has gone against Israel in any way, it has caused disaster such as floods, storms, hurricanes, and so on.

That's the way it will be. Israel shall prevail.

It reminded me of what my friend Morris said years ago when we were talking the way someone at work was treating a mutual Christian friend of ours. He said "They gonna pay for that. You can't get away with doing God's people wrong."

That's so true.

Coffee and Prayers

There will always be attacks upon God's people. And they will always fail. Many people will attack, falsely accuse, and try to destroy God's people. They will lie, make false reports, and do anything to try and gain victory. God, however, filters all through His hands. We also last week saw this in the election.

If you're being persecuted, attacked by your enemies, then take heart. God sees it all. He knows the evil plans that people plot against His people. He sees the contempt that the unjust show for His word.

Take heart and pray daily. Make His word your guide. Comfort yourself in His promises. Have a great day everyone.

"'If it had not been the Lord who was on our side,' Let Israel now say—'If it had not been the Lord who was on our side, When men rose up against us, Then they would have swallowed us alive, When their wrath was kindled against us; Then the waters would have overwhelmed us, The stream would have gone over our soul; Then the swollen waters Would have gone over our soul." Blessed be the Lord, Who has not given us as prey to their teeth. Our soul has escaped as a bird from the snare of the fowlers; The snare is broken, and we have escaped. Our help is in the name of the Lord, Who made heaven and earth.'" Psalm 124:1-8

Coffee and Prayers this Cool Friday Morning.

The weekend is finally here.

One of the most famous biblical stories of the outstanding wisdom of King Solomon, which won the expression "The Judgment of Solomon" relates to the clever tactic by which Solomon resolved a literally unsolvable dispute. The story related in Kings 3:16-28, tells of two prostitutes who came before King Solomon, bringing with them a single Babyboy.

Each mother told the same story: that they both lived together, that both had given birth to a child, that one child was dead in the morning and that the live child was hers. Each mother accused the other, that after having discovered that her child had died during the night, its mother had stolen the other mother's live baby and replaced it with the dead child. Thus, each mother claimed, on waking up in the morning, she had discovered a dead child on her breast, which was not hers.

Coffee and Prayers

In a dispute such as this, where there is no evidence or witness, King Solomon's solution is fascinating. After some deliberation, he called for a sword to be brought before him. He declared that there was only one fair solution, namely, that the live child should be split in two, each woman receiving half of the child. Upon hearing this terrible verdict, the baby's true mother cried out in horror and anguish, "Please, My Lord, give her the live child - do not kill him!" However, the liar, in her bitter jealousy, exclaimed, "It shall be neither mine nor yours - divide it!" Realizing that a true mother's instincts are to protect her child, Solomon instantly gave the baby to the real mother, who was willing to relinquish her baby in order to save its life.

In our day and time, we see so many times that people would rather destroy another life to "keep" it, rather than to relinquish it. We see news stories of jealous and spiteful people who kill a wife or husband, girlfriend or boyfriend if they "can't have him or her."

There are people who will absolutely prefer seeing their family, friends, parents, siblings, children, or whoever else gets in their way "cut in half" rather than admit they are wrong.

Coffee and Prayers

It's truly sad that it's like that. People will do that to themselves as well.

We see it many times.

Satan is especially like that. He wants everyone. All of us. He wants the worship that only God is worthy of. So when he can't have someone, he sets out to destroy them. The lost, the atheists, the Satanists, and all of those who worship false gods, they pose no threat to him. They may say they don't believe in God, the devil, heaven or hell. But that doesn't mean none of them exist. They are, by default, a child of the devil. Not making a choice means that it's made for you. Just as the two women didn't lay claim to the dead child, neither does Satan lay claim to those who are dead in their lostness.

They are his already.

It was the live child whom both the women laid claim to, and Solomon, in his God given wisdom, knew how to bring out who was the TRUE mother. The one who would rather let another have him than to see him brutally cut in half.

God takes the approach that He'd sacrifice His own Son on the cross, letting Him take our sins, rather than see us "cut in half", and both pieces go to the devil. He let His Son suffer, die, and be buried and raised again to show how much He loves us.

Some, no many will reject Christ.

These are the ones who Satan doesn't look to destroy. He already has them. It's those who are in Christ whom he seeks to destroy. He wants to place fear, doubt, anger, and everything else to make us doubt God and His promise. He wants us cut in half. Are you a child of the Living God? If so, then nothing can truly come against you without being filtered through His hands. If you are truly saved, then there is nothing that can change that. Nothing. There won't be any "cutting you in half". You are and always will be fully and wholly HIS. Consider these verses, and have a great day everyone.

"'My Father, who has given them to Me, is greater than all; and no one is able to snatch them out of My Father's hand. I and My Father are one.'" John 10:29-30

Coffee and Prayers

Coffee and Prayers this Beautiful Monday Morning.

Several years ago at a family gathering, my late brother in law's sister was lamenting the fact that she couldn't "find a good man." I asked her where she was looking, and she went on to say that she doesn't go anywhere or do anything. I suggested that she perhaps go to church, join a small group, or maybe do some volunteer work. She then said that she just didn't "have the energy" to do anything. I suggested that she start exercising, just start by walking short distances and walk a little more each day. Every suggestion I had, she shot down with some excuse. I then told her that unless good men were going door to door, she had no chance. I then told her that if she always did what she'd always done, she'd always get what she'd always got.

The fact is, no one will ever meet anyone if their house is their prison.

It's the same way with anything in life. We can pray and pray, but we also must take steps ourselves.

God, all through the Bible, has worked many things out, but it took action on our parts as well. God spared Noah and his family and the animals, but Noah had to work 120 years building the ark. God freed the children of Israel, but it took actions on their part, and even 40 years of wandering to complete it. God delivered the philistine giant into David's hands, but it took an effort on David's part as well. Jesus worked many miracles, but it took faith and an effort. Peter had to cast his nets to catch the fish Jesus told him he'd catch.

We have to pray, and take an action. In my brother in law's sister's case, she may have been praying for a "good man", but God wasn't going to send one to her door most likely. If we want a job, we pray and we search. If we want to improve our house, we pray and paint and repair! If we are sick, we pray and we go to the doctor.

We must have faith as all those in the Bible did. God didn't build the ark FOR Noah. He didn't just teleport Israel out of Egypt. He didn't just cause the philistine giant to drop dead.

That what we need must be prayed for and acted upon.

If we always do what we've always done, we will always get what we've always got.

Pray continuously and ask God what steps it is you must take and then take them. Have a great day everyone.

Coffee and Prayers

"What does it profit, my brethren, if someone says he has faith but does not have works? Can faith save him? If a brother or sister is naked and destitute of daily food, and one of you says to them, "Depart in peace, be warmed and filled," but you do not give them the things which are needed for the body, what does it profit? Thus also faith by itself, if it does not have works, is dead." James 2: 14-17

Coffee and Prayers this Cool Tuesday Morning.

Clouds are rolling in from the south this morning.

The quiet cool before dawn is a stark contrast to the noise and chaos the day will hold. I saw a couple of things yesterday about "earth day" and couldn't help but be amused. I smiled because there are people who believe that all of this recycling and so forth started in the 70's in all of the "save the earth" movements. The fact is that I remember my grandparents recycled everything that they could. Not in a "save the earth" state of mind, but in a "being a good steward of what God has given us" state of mind. They re-used, recycled, used up, fixed, fixed again and again, and wore out everything until they got every possible last use out of it. They believed in treating every single thing as a good gift from God and not wasting it. My grandparents were not wealthy. They came up in the depression. Their parents and grandparents had long before a depression instilled good stewardship in them.

My Dad talks about how his parents and uncles and other family members would save nails that were bent, and on some days would sit there and take a hammer and straighten the bent nails to re-use. To simply throw them away wasn't heard of. Everything that could possibly be re-used was re-used. I have had people laugh when I talk about how meals were saved and reheated day after day until they were all eaten up. There was no throwing out food. People will say it's being "cheap". It's simply being a good steward of what God has provided. Taking care of our homes, our cars, our clothes, our furniture, every single thing that we are given is simply to show respect and gratitude to that which we have been blessed with.

Being wasteful simply is not wise.

When I turn out lights and turn off water running unnecessarily, I am not trying to be miserly; I am simply trying to save water and electricity. I would much rather have the money in my pocket than to be paying it to the power company or water company, etc. It's not a matter of being "stingy". It's not stinginess or greed when we simply make the most use out of all that weave and get the most use out of what God has given us. It shows honor to God when we show appreciation for all His gifts, no matter how small. We show appreciation by getting the most use from them and wasting not even a tiny portion. Have a great day everyone. "The plans of the diligent lead sure to plenty, but those of everyone who is hasty, surely to poverty." Proverbs 21:5

Coffee and Prayers this Cool Wednesday Morning.

Federal Express (FedEx). It's a household word. One of the most recognized companies in the world. Started by a man named Fred Smith.

The company is truly a remarkable entity. Its reputation is built upon the capability to deliver a letter or package overnight. Anywhere. Anywhere in the world. I can place a letter or package into a FedEx box in Memphis, and it can be in Beijing China tomorrow. I can send one from Kuwait to Kansas overnight. It doesn't matter.

The World Headquarters and super hub of FedEx in Memphis is a sprawling, gigantic testimony to this

Coffee and Prayers

company. Hangars, planes, trucks. Hundreds of offices and work areas. Over 400,000 employees worldwide. Nearly 700planes from giant Airbuses to small "feeder" planes. Thousands of trucks and vans worldwide. They even have their own police department.

I've been in the facilities in Memphis many times.

I've seen employees working away in offices; I've seen them outside on breaks and in the many cafeterias enjoying lunch. Never once did I wonder, "Now how is THAT person sitting there getting my package or letter to _____?" Yet somehow they are connected to it. If I drop a letter in a FedEx collection box early this morning, I can stand there all day and worry and fret over it arriving on time to where I'm sending it. I may think it's never going to make it because it's now later in the afternoon and it's STILL SITTING HERE IN THE BOX! However, before a certain time, it will be collected, along with the others and sent on its way. I can go online and track its movements. I can even be texted when it arrives.

So, back to all the seemingly chaotic happenings at the Headquarters in Memphis. What do all those employees have to do with my letter, and what is my point? Well, my point is this. Why should I worry about the "chaos" at Headquarters? Why should I concern myself with employees who seem to have no interest in my letter still in the collection box? Well, I have the FedEx guarantee of overnight delivery. And so it's like this with our life. If we are saved, we shouldn't be worried about the "chaos." We shouldn't be worried about these "roadblocks" to God's promise to us. Why? Because of His WORD. That's why.

Many hundreds of things that are seemingly unrelated to my letter at FedEx are going on. Yet, each is related to it in some way.

Many things are happening in life that are seemingly unrelated to what God promised, yet somehow related.

I heard a woman on "Focus on the Family" the other day relate this. Her daughter was on the woman's laptop and accidentally downloaded a virus, a ransom ware virus. She had an entire book she'd written on that laptop and it was due at the publisher in just days. She got a computer tech involved and he was able to transfer all her information onto an external hard drive.

Then, 2 days later her laptop was stolen. Had she not had the virus, she'd never have a back-up for her book!

So, that all worked out according to God's plan. (If I recall correctly, the title of her book is "Unglued " by Lysa TerKeurst on how to deal with everyday problems in life without becoming emotionally unglued.) So, when something comes up in our lives, and it seems as if chaos is reigning, remember His Word. Remember that HE is in charge. HE has the pieces in place to make sure everything works out.

Also remember that God doesn't wear a watch. He doesn't own a Clock. He doesn't own a Calendar. He works things out with timing, not time.

It is not important for us to know how every little thing is going to fit into place to work things out. It is only important that we know that God has placed everything in place to make it work out.

Have a great day everyone.

"And we know that all things work together for good to those who love God, to those who are the called according to His purpose." Romans 8:28

Coffee and Prayers

Coffee and Prayers this Cool Wednesday Morning.

I thought about one of the movies I never get tired of watching, "Jaws". I've made a couple of posts about this movie, but so many parallels to life can be made. One scene I was thinking about was where shark expert Matt Hooper and Police Chief Martin Brody were trying to convince Mayor Vaughn to close the beaches, because a great white shark, a giant great white, had staked his territory there at Amity Island. A 25 foot, 3 ton great white. The mayor refused, because it was the July 4th weekend, and business depended upon tourist dollars being spend there at the beach at Amity.

Matt Hooper tells the Mayor, "The Great White is an eating machine. All it does is swim, and eat, and make little sharks." He tried explaining that the great white would remain unless it was killed, or its food supply cut off. It had already killed several people, and even had sunk a boat. Hooper's point was (and I'm adding this) that there was no reasoning with the shark. The shark had this behavior in its DNA. Of course the mayor couldn't be reasoned with either. The mayor stubbornly refused to make the tough choice to save lives. He kept the beaches open, and of course the shark attacked again, and killed again. The mayor finally agreed to sign the papers to pay to have the shark killed. The mayor's kids had been on that very beach where the shark had attacked. His kids could have been killed. Some people are like that in life. They stubbornly refuse to listen to truth, to facts, to the warnings.

They only see what they want to see.

They refuse to listen to reason. Much like Mayor Vaughn in the movie, they see only what will benefit THEM at the moment. Vaughn saw dollars for Amity, which would of course mean votes for him. Closing the beaches would mean lost revenue and angry constituents. It could also cost him his future as mayor. He put money and his own interests above the safety of the town, although he claimed that he was acting in the town's best interest. People are that way when it comes to many things, not the least of which is their relationship with God. They want a "short term pleasure", desire, whatever.

They refuse to see the danger.

Be it their salvation, or be it a refusal to listen to reason about a relationship and restoring it, forgiveness, or anything else. They simply are like that shark. They refuse to see what's best for themselves, their marriage, their children, their parents. They do their thing and that's all. They are like Mayor Vaughn. They see short term benefit and that's all. They can't be reasoned with. It took the mayor having his kids in extreme danger to open his eyes and do the right thing. The shark had to be hunted down and finally killed.

So what about us in real life?

Do we have something that is so important to us that we would endanger ourselves? Our families? Our kids? Our relationships? Our fellowship with God? Do we stubbornly refuse to listen to reason? Do we stubbornly refuse to see the dangers? Do we refuse the counsel of the wise? Have you ever lived through some things, experienced the consequences of your sin, and try to convince someone whom you see doing that very thing just blow off your advice, your counsel, your word of warning? Sin is much worse than a 3 ton great white. The enemy is constantly looking for anyone to devour. We either cut off the Devils "food supply", or we will put ourselves or others in danger.

Please listen to reason.

Please listen to those who offer wise counsel. Don't compromise when it comes to His word. Don't be as that fictional mayor and only open your eyes

when it is too late. Have a great day everyone.
"'Come now, and let us reason together, 'Says the Lord, 'Though your sins are like scarlet, They shall be as white as snow; Though they are red like crimson, They shall be as wool. If you are willing and obedient, you shall eat the good of the land; But if you refuse and rebel, you shall be devoured by the sword'; for the mouth of the Lord has spoken. Isaiah 1:18-20

Coffee and Prayers this Cold Wednesday Morning.

I was thinking about how when I was a kid, if the weather wasn't where I could play outside, I would often either be inside reading either the encyclopedia or comic books.

I remember one summer I was out at my Grandma's house. I was reading a comic book and was noticing the always present ads from the "Johnson-Smith Company." They advertised things from "X-Ray glasses" to books on how to be a ventriloquist. There was also an ad for a "live animal trap". I wanted this trap to catch squirrels and all alive.

Coffee and Prayers

I cut out the ad and wrote down the item number for this trap, enclosed my $2.98 or whatever it was and mailed it off. I watched the mail every week, and then one day the mailman, Mr. Vernon Leman, brought me not a box, but an envelope. Inside the envelope was my "trap." The trap was 3 plastic sticks, one with a flat end. They had to be joined together as to form a "4", and placed under a heavy box (not included of course). The flat part was to be baited and when the animal would come eat the bait, it was supposed to cause the box to fall on it trapping it.

I of course was very disappointed. I even tried to see if it might work, but I could never get it to.

I wrote a letter to the company and returned it for a refund, which to my dismay was not cash, but postage stamps! Lesson learned.

Many years later one of my daughters came home from the Mid-South Fair with an extremely tall "tropical drink" glass. It had a stem that must have been a foot tall. She was so excited that she had "only paid $8 for so much to drink!"

I smiled and said "Let me show you something." We went into the kitchen and I filled this huge tropical drink glass with water. I then poured it into one of our kitchen glasses. It barely filled it. That large drink glass barely held 12 ounces, for which she paid $8 for. She was upset that she had been cheated.

As I think of these two relatively innocuous events, I think about how Eskimos sometimes catch wolves. A sharp knife will be dipped in seal blood and the blood will freeze to the blade. The knife is then stuck into the ground with only the bloody blade exposed. A wolf, attracted to the smell of the blood will then begin to lick the blood from the frozen blade. With its tongue, numbed by the cold blade, the wolf never realizes its tongue is sliced open and that the warm, fresh blood that it is now consuming is indeed its own. It will continue until it dies.

That's the way sin is.

It will advertise something that is so "great". It will make you think you are getting a bargain. I twill deceive you into spending way more than something is worth.

That business man on that trip far from home thinks that the one night stand with the cutie in the bar is a bargain. Then a trip to the doctor reveals that it wasn't a bargain at all.

Coffee and Prayers

The woman who thinks she's getting a "bargain" by having the affair with her also married coworker. Then all is revealed and two families are destroyed.

The teen who thinks that "Mr. Wonderful" is a bargain, until she ends up pregnant. The teen who thinks that a few drugs are a bargain until there is an addiction or an overdose.

That person who thinks that that person, boyfriend or girlfriend, or whoever, who tried to destroy them who threw them to the wolves, betrayed them, is now somehow a "bargain." A bargain until they are right back in their circle and will betray them again.

Satan is the ultimate liar, the ultimate deceiver. And let's face it. Much of sin is a pleasure to most people. The Bible even says so. (Hebrews 11:24-25 By faith Moses, when he became of age, refused to be called the son of Pharaoh's daughter, choosing rather to suffer affliction with the people of God than to enjoy the passing pleasures of sin...)
If it wasn't, not many would commit them.

However, we, much like the wolves that the Eskimo hunts, greedily consume our own blood, unaware that we are killing ourselves.

Coffee and Prayers

We have to be careful that we aren't letting the enemy sell us something that is not what it is supposed to be. We must take care that we use the Bible as our guide, and we must pray daily for wisdom. We must ask the Holy Spirit to stay within us. We at best end up could end up paying way more than something is worth, or at worst end up as the wolf, consuming our own blood, killing ourselves. As I've heard it said before, sin will carry you further than you want to go, keep you longer than you wanted to stay, and cost you more than you wanted to pay.

We do have someone who has paid it all for us. When we are His, He gives us back that which is lost, redeems us, and cleanses us. Have a great day everyone.

"'Come now, and let us reason together," Says the Lord, "Though your sins are like scarlet, They shall be as white as snow; Though they are red like crimson, They shall be as wool. If you are willing and obedient, You shall eat the good of the land;'" Isaiah 1:18-19

Coffee and Prayers

Coffee and Prayers this Freezing Cold New Year's Day.

I've looked around for an old movie I'd like to see again.

It came out in 1980 titled "Touched by Love". It is the true story of a young girl named Karen, played by a very young Diane Lane in the movie. Karen had cerebral palsy and was confined to a wheelchair. The story takes place in the60's. She was abandoned by her mother in a group home for the disabled. Karen was withdrawn and very unfriendly and bitter.

A nurse named Lena spent a lot of time trying to coax Karen out of her shell. She tried everything. She was frustrated at every turn. Then one day when they had some of the patients in town for an outing, Karen indicated that she wanted bubble gum. "Oh, you like bubble gum?" Lena asked her. Karen shook her head no. "But you want bubblegum?" Lena asked again. Karen nodded her head yes. "You don't like bubble gum but you want bubble gum?" Karen again nodded yes.

An aide (portrayed by John Amos) who pushed Karen's wheelchair smiled and said "Just a typical woman!"

Coffee and Prayers

A little later, Lena happened to notice that Karen would sit in her chair and hold something close to her tightly. It was the cards that came with her gum, cards with pictures of Elvis Presley.

Lena wasn't exactly a fan of Elvis, but when she finally coaxed it out of Karen that she really loved Elvis; she knew that she had a way to reach her. One of the highlights of her life was getting to go to see Elvis' latest movie.

Karen then asked if she could write a letter to her idol. Lena agreed and Karen explained in her letter that she had cerebral palsy, lived in a group home, and so forth. They mailed the letter and excitedly awaited a return letter from Elvis.

The days turned into weeks with no reply. The weeks marched on. Karen began to recede back into her shell, saddened that Elvis didn't write back. This of course didn't endear Lena to him as she saw all of her progress with Karen fade away.

Then one day it wasn't a letter that arrived, it was a huge box addressed to Karen. It was a box full of Elvis albums, records, autographed pictures for Karen, and other Elvis memorabilia. There was also a hand-written letter from Elvis, apologizing for taking so long to reply. He explained that he had been on location filming his next movie, and he

Coffee and Prayers

gave her an address to write him so that her letters would come straight to him!

Karen and Elvis became pen-pals, and Karen was happier than she had ever been in her life. They wrote back and forth, and Elvis always sent her gifts such as his latest records and pictures. Lena was ecstatic that Karen had come out of her shell at last.

Then Elvis one day wrote that he would like to come and visit Karen soon after he finished his next movie. This was of course the best news that Karen had ever had in her life. She was so happy!

Then a few days later, Lena went into Karen's room to discover that she had died in her sleep a few days before Elvis' visit.

A bittersweet ending no doubt. However Lena had never given up on trying reaching Karen, despite the objections of the head of the group home. Although she died at an early age, Karen did die knowing that she was loved, and loved in return.

We never know what it will take to tear down a wall that someone has built up over the years. Sometimes it takes never giving up, watching them closely, and encouraging that which they hold as important.

Coffee and Prayers

Supposed Lena had just decided that Karen wasn't worth the time and effort and was a hopeless cause as the head of the group home determined. Karen would have died a lonely, bitter child who had felt no love from anyone.

Everyone has worth, everyone has value, no matter how isolated, how bitter, how closed off they may seem, they have worth and are worthy of love. Isn't it great to know that our Savior looks at us in that way? When others look at us as not worthy of their time or love, He reaches out to us and uses things and people to reach us and show us the light of His salvation in ways that we could never even imagine.

He will never give up on us. Even when the world and those in it kicks us to the curb, makes us feel unwanted and unloved, He is always there, showing us that we were worthy enough for Him to die for.

We are worthy because HE determined that we are worthy. And what He determines is all that counts.

Have a great day everyone, and a happy and prosperous new year, with all the Lord's blessings.

"For I know the thoughts that I think toward you, says the Lord, thoughts of peace and not of evil, to give you a future and a hope. Then you will call upon Me and go and pray to Me, and I will listen to you. And you will seek Me and find Me, when you search for Me with all your heart." Jeremiah 29:11-13

Coffee and Prayers this Monday Morning.

I was online one day, looking at something I was thinking of buying. I was looking at the ratings, and how this product had a 99% satisfaction rating. Pretty good, right? When I see similar ratings on products and services I can't help but think about that other 1%. If a company has a million customers, then one hundred thousand were NOT satisfied.

Stats can be very good indexes on such things. And of course it's nearly impossible for any person or company to provide 100% customer satisfaction. So what happens to the 1%?

Does God care about us when our faith wains and we tend to wander away? There are millions and millions of those faithful who are still serving, still faithful, still right there. So is God satisfied with having the 99% still there? Does He just "write off" the others?

Coffee and Prayers

When we just withdraw into ourselves and away from even Him, what does God do?

A couple of years ago, Cindy told me that when she was keeping one of our granddaughters, she taught her from Matthew 18:12-13. Jesus said "What do you think? If a man has a hundred sheep, and one of them goes astray, does he not leave the ninety-nine and go to the mountains to seek the one that is straying? And if he should find it, Assuredly, I say to you, he rejoices more over that sheep than over the ninety-nine that did not go astray." Jesus considers us HIS SHEEP. He is our Shepherd.

Cindy taught her that "He will leave the 99 to come and get you." I still picture her telling her that, and I pray that sweet little girl always remembers that. I pray that everyone remembers that.

Have you gone astray? Have you dropped out of church, stopped praying, stopped believing? Has work, career, obligations, and other life events just caused you to be distracted and caused you to just wander away? Do you think He doesn't care? If you think so, you've bought into a lie straight from hell.

God isn't satisfied with 99%. He sent His Son to die for us. He wants ALL of His sheep with Him. He loves us all. Know that He is your Shepherd. He will bring you back, hold you in His arms, clean you up, and rejoice over you .You are not in some "1%". You are HIS 100%. Have a great day everyone.

"But, beloved, do not forget this one thing, that with the Lord one day is as a thousand years, and a thousand years as one day. The Lord is not slack concerning His promise, as some count slackness, but is longsuffering toward us, not willing that any should perish but that all should come to repentance." 2 Peter 3:8-9

Coffee and Prayers, and after what seems like an Eternity, Finally Friday.

A couple of years ago I heard about two young ladies who had rented a house in Memphis. They were roommates and had, between school and work, spent a couple of days painting and settling in.

They had only been there a few days when about 1:00am one morning they heard banging on their door. It scared them, and they looked out the window and saw several Memphis Police officers.

It turns out that the neighbors had been calling for months about the people who had lived in the house previously! They'd called for months, they'd gotten no response. Now two innocent young girls lived there, they'd not bothered anyone, and the police show up! The commotion woke the neighbors who came over and explained to police.

That's the way life is sometimes.

When seconds count, help is only months away.

So what about God's timing? How quickly does HE respond? Well, that depends. We may think that we are out of time, but God bases His response on TIMING, not TIME. God sees the end as He sees the beginning. He's not guessing at what His response should be. He knows when and How He should show Himself. How many times in life do we think "If God had only…" Or "I'm sure glad that God didn't…"

When the end is there, we can always see that He did or didn't do a certain thing because He knows the outcome.

Are you waiting for Him?

He's delaying because it's what is going to be what is best for you. It may not seem like it now, but you will see in the end. He's not like humans who "drop the ball" and show up a day late and a dollar short.

His timing will be perfect for you. Your back may be to the sea with Pharaoh's army bearing down on you. When you're at the end of your rope, tie a knot in it and hang on. God is going to show Himself in a mighty way. Think of the testimony you'll have then!

Have a great day everyone.

"Thus says the Lord: 'In an acceptable time I have heard you, and in the day of salvation I have helped you; I will preserve you...'" Isaiah 49:8

Coffee and Prayers this Thursday Morning.

The weekend is in sight, just keep walking towards it.

Last night I was thinking about a small group fish fry that we had about 12 years ago at the Cothern's home.

We just decided to cook some fish and have some fellowship time outside of our usual small group dynamics. There were a lot of people there outside of our "group", and we were about to eat when

Coffee and Prayers

two well-dressed ladies walked in .They looked around a little nervously, and everyone told them to come on in , grab a plate and help themselves to fish , hush puppies , fries , and all the rest . As they nervously looked around they began asking "Are you related to so and so or so and so?" No one had a clue who it was they were talking about. And as they asked more questions, they looked more confused. Finally one of the ladies asked "Is this the so and so wedding reception?" Of course it wasn't. What had happened was that someone had told them to go down into the neighborhood and look for all the cars.

We invited them to stay and eat with us anyway. They were clearly tempted to do just that. They were embarrassed at their mistake, but were in awe of the hospitality they were shown here. Two strangers who were treated as friends, as family.

Christian love demonstrated to two strangers. They perhaps talk of it today, how they were treated by a group of people who had no idea who they were, yet welcomed them with open arms.

We have to be leery of strangers no doubt. And it's no doubt that when I see someone I don't know, a group of people walk into a store or other place I'm in, I've already made a "threat assessment" of them. It's just a soldier/cop thing.

It's a balance between vigilance and showing kindness.

It's a fine line at times. God knows your heart. Sometimes just a smile, a "good morning", holding a door open will make someone's bad day just a little better. Make someone's day today. Show them the kindness you'd like to receive. Have a great day everyone.

"Let brotherly love continue. Do not forget to entertain strangers, for by so doing some have unwittingly entertained angels." Hebrews 13:1-2

Coffee and Prayers this very Rainy Wednesday Morning.

I was talking to a relative one day a couple of years ago.

She has a friend who was, she feared, being scammed by someone online claiming to be an American soldier deployed in Afghanistan (or somewhere) and needed cash to "register his fiancée".

She sent me pics of all the documents that this faker was using so that I could take a look. The "fiancée registration form" I could tell right away was a fake. First of all, there is no such thing.

The form states that once "registered ", the fiancée is entitled to all benefits, etc. In the military you are married or not. There isn't anything in between. Also, the "fee" for registering (300 -700) was listed in pounds instead of dollars. Their "official" email address was an @AOL .com. All military emails have a .mil address, and the government has a .gov address. All official army forms are "DA" forms; all general military forms are "DD" forms. Of course this form had neither.

Then there was his so called passport. Individuals who are on orders overseas get no charge passports, but a military deployment doesn't warrant passports. In any case, his "passport" had several problems. The first thing I noticed was the passport ID pic. This "soldier" was wearing a Desert Storm era uniform along with a boonie hat. Hats aren't allowed in ID pics. The pic was not even a straight on shot, it was at an angle. Obviously it was not taken as an ID pic. Not to mention that it said "United STATE of America" instead of United

Coffee and Prayers

STATES. Needless to say, this was all as bogus as a 3 dollar bill.

I know what fake soldiers look like because I know what real ones look like. I know what fake ID cards look like because I know what real ID cards look like.

It's easy to spot anything fake, phony, or counterfeit if you know what the real thing looks like.

Bank tellers are trained to spot fake bills, checks and all and are trained to know what real ones look like. They know what a real one looks like so a fake is easy, most times, to spot.

Jewelers can spot fake diamonds because they know what real ones look like.

People can be suckered into believing many things as long as it "looks real".

Scams occur every day. Crooks and con artists take advantage of people two ways. They take advantage of either their greed, or their generosity. The greedy will believe that email that stated that they've won some contest that they never entered. They will send all their information, or some "fee" to pay to have this phony prize awarded.

Coffee and Prayers

The generous, such as my cousin's friend, will feel sorry for some sob story such as a deployed soldier needing cash to "register their fiancée".

So what about spotting something fake that someone reads or is told about our relationship with Christ?

Is that really Biblical what that person said? What that person wrote? Well there is one way to tell, and that is to know God's word.

Someone says "You don't HAVE to forgive", or "it's okay to steal", or hundreds of other things that someone may believe. Some will say that God had changed His mind to suit society.
Some will believe that they can be mean, nasty, hateful, vindictive, selfish, and just basically live as they wish to out of their greed and they will be okay as long as they just throw God's name out there now and then.

Then there are those who, out of a misguided sense of compassion will try to help some along in their sin, believing that they shouldn't tell them the truth of their errors. They become an "enabler" of someone's sin or even their own.

Coffee and Prayers

Why? Well those who act out of greed basically want to bring God down to their level. They care nothing about truth; they only want to get all they can out of life, no matter the manner they do it in.

Those who act out of compassion, they just don't want to be confrontational perhaps. Or maybe they just don't know the truth in either case.

We all sin, we all sin daily. But when it's a blatant lifestyle, then we have to examine our hearts. Are we just thumbing our noses at God? Or are we just ignorant to the truth?

Knowing the truth is life. Satan depends upon our inability to discern what is fake and what is real. If he can use greed to get us to fall, he will. He will use anything he can to get us out of fellowship with God if we are saved, or anything he can to keep us from salvation if we are not saved.

The truth. Being able to discern truth and knowing what is REAL will keep us from getting scammed by people, and it will keep us from being scammed by the devil.

Knowledge. Knowledge of truth, discernment of truth, knowing what is real and what is not. That's what we must strive for daily. Have a great day everyone.

Coffee and Prayers

"Yes, if you cry out for discernment, And lift up your voice for understanding, If you seek her as silver, And search for her as for hidden treasures; Then you will understand the fear of the Lord, And find the knowledge of God. For the

Lord gives wisdom; From His mouth come knowledge and understanding; He stores up sound wisdom for the upright; He is a shield to those who walk uprightly; He guards the paths of justice, And preserves the way of His saints. Then you will understand righteousness and justice, Equity and every good path. When wisdom enters your heart, And knowledge is pleasant to your soul, Discretion will preserve you; Understanding will keep you, To deliver you from the way of evil, From the man who speaks perverse things, From those who leave the paths of uprightness To walk in the ways of darkness; Who rejoice in doing evil, And delight in the perversity of the wicked; Whose ways are crooked, And who are devious in their paths; To deliver you from the immoral woman, From the seductress who flatters with her words, Who forsakes the companion of her youth, And forgets the covenant of her God. For her house leads down to death, And her paths to the dead;" Proverbs 2:3-18

Coffee and Prayers

Coffee and Prayers this Christmas Eve.

I had said my prayers and was praying with Cindy, Zoog decided to come lick me right in the face!

This morning, something came to me that I hadn't thought about in a while. Several years ago

I was interviewing a man for a position with my team. As I asked him different questions, I noticed how he would cut his eyes to look at the Bible verse that I kept on a bulletin board in my office.

After answering all my questions honestly, candidly, and without hesitation, I asked him if there's anything about himself he'd like to add.

He said "I notice your Bible verse, so I assume you're a Christian and so am I."

He then quoted Isaiah 54:2

"Enlarge the place of your tent, And let them stretch out the curtains of your dwellings..."

He told me of how he prayed that daily, and that how he believed he was led to my team. And that verse I had reaffirmed that he was in the right place.

Coffee and Prayers

I did end up hiring him, and he was a good addition. I had no problem giving good recommendations on him years later when others would call me and ask me about him.

So how are we each praying daily? Are we somehow afraid to ask God to bless us? Are we of the mindset that we aren't worthy of His blessings?

I alone am not. But it's Jesus in me that alone makes me worthy. It's His GRACE that gives us that which we aren't worthy of. Are you afraid to ask Him? I don't mean trying to use God as you would Amazon, and just assume that He will ship you anything you put on your wish list. I mean asking Him out of a heart for Him. Asking Him for blessings and protection. Asking Him for wisdom and guidance.

It's like what I've told one of our daughters. Psalm 37:4 "Delight yourself also in the Lord, And He shall give you the desires of your heart."

Also Matthew 6:33 "But seek first the kingdom of God and His righteousness, and all these things shall be added to you."

As I told her, these aren't my words, they are HIS.

Coffee and Prayers

The man who sat in my office had prayed, had sought HIM first, and a position with my team was a boon to his career. I was more than willing to give him a position, and never regretted it.

What is it that you have desire for? If it's wealth and material things only, or first even, there's a good chance that you will have these, but at a price.

"For what will it profit a man if he gains the whole world, and loses his own soul?"
Mark8:36

But when we seek HIM first, His Word says that these things will be added to us.

What is it you seek? What is it you trust in? Is it wealth? Position?

When our hearts are right towards Him, we can pray and have faith that He will hear us. And He will give to us that which will bless us.

What is it you seek this Christmas? What is it you seek in the New Year that is a week away?

What was the Bible verse that I had on my bulletin board that reaffirmed this young man that he was seeking correctly? I'll close with it. Also, have a great day and a Merry Christmas.

"And Jabez called on the God of Israel saying, 'Oh, that You would bless me indeed, and enlarge my territory, that Your hand would be with me, and that You would keep me from evil, that I may not cause pain!' So God granted him what he requested." 1 Chronicles 4:10

Coffee and Prayers this Freezing Cold New Year's Day.

On New Year's, most people are looking forward, looking ahead. They make "resolutions "on how they plan to change their lives in the coming year. One day Cindy and I were discussing motorcycles. Bikes as us biker types call them. Anyway, I was telling her about how when someone is a passenger (I won't use the biker term for passenger), they have to fully trust the driver. (Her first ride with me a few years ago, by the way, she rode like an expert. As if she'd been riding all her life.)

Coffee and Prayers

For example, a novice rider will sometimes panic during a turn. This is because in a turn, the bars aren't actually turned; a bike is leaned into the turn. On a left turn, the driver leans the bike over to his left, a right turn, to the right. The bars are rarely turned, and the front wheel mostly stays in a straight line with the rest of the bike. The handlebars are turned only when maneuvering in tight spots. The bars are turned only a few degrees 99% of the time.

A passenger will sometimes panic when the bike leans way over. Their nature is to try to stay "upright". This can really mess the driver up, as the driver needs the passenger to lean with the bike.

The passenger must fully trust the driver of the bike.

If they don't lean when they should, it can end up bad. The driver sees the curves ahead, and he always anticipates them and readies for them.

Such is life. We will have all sorts of curves and turns in life. When we are riding with God, and we don't fully trust Him, and we don't lean in the curves with Him, we can scare ourselves to death. We can never crash God's will, but we can sure make the trip bad for ourselves. Experienced passengers on a bike look as relaxed as if they're at

Coffee and Prayers

home on their couch. You can tell a new passenger, because they are fidgety, squirming in the seat, and so on. They can make the ride miserable.

When we do this with God, not trusting Him to take the curves and deliver us safely, we cancel out our faith with our fear. We make the curves harder than they have to be.

Leaning a big 900 pound bike way over at 50, 60, or 70 miles an hour or faster can be a thrill if you have faith, terrifying if you're in fear.

If we are trusting God, we can lean with Him so far over that our knees almost scrape the pavement and we won't crash.

No matter what curves, no matter how sharp the turns. God sees the end as the beginning. No curve is unexpected for Him.

He's been "riding passengers" since He created Adam. He hasn't crashed yet and never will.
We can just hold on and trust Him.

Have a great day everyone. Lean with those curves!

"For I know the thoughts that I think toward you, says the Lord, thoughts of peace and not of evil, to give you a future and a hope." Jeremiah 29:11

Coffee and Prayers

Coffee and Prayers this Already Hot and Sticky Wednesday Morning.

Last night I was thinking about a time several years ago. I had just started at Coca-Cola, and there was a young man who worked there who came up as we were all talking one morning. He asked me if I was still in the rodeo circuit. I asked him what he was talking about. He said "You're a saddle bronc rider." I replied that I had no idea what he was talking about. I told him that I GO to the rodeo every year, but I'm not a rider. He argued "Yes you are, I've seen you. You ride saddle broncs." I told him that I have never rode in a rodeo in my life. He became even more adamant about it. "I've SEEN YOU in the rodeo. I've WATCHED you ride saddle broncs!" "You may have SEEN SOMEONE ride saddle broncs in the rodeo" I replied ,"but I assure you, you've never seen ME do it."

He was becoming agitated by this time and kept insisting that he knew what he was talking about. I finally, as a joke, said "The last time I was even on a horse, it threw me, my leg got caught in the stirrup, and I may have been seriously hurt had the manager of Piggly Wiggly not come out and unplugged it!" Everyone fell out laughing. He walked away angry.

Coffee and Prayers

Has that ever happened to you? Someone INSISTS that you've done or said something and they were just flat out wrong about it? Maybe they were misinformed. Maybe they believed something that someone told them, or maybe they just made it up.

People will try to define others by what they've heard about them. Most of the time it will be rumor, gossip, and lies told by a person or persons who has so little in life, they want to drag others down. They want to "define" you. They want to define you to others.

No matter what our story is, someone somewhere is changing it to suit them.

It's just part of life I suppose.

Someone who is bitter, angry, or just mean, will whisper behind the back of the single mom, behind the back of the divorcee, behind the back of the person who is trying to turn his or her life around.

There will be those who want to define us in THEIR terms.

The enemy will try this every day. He will try to define us by our past. But when we are saved, we are defined by who God says we are and the FUTURE that He has for us.

Coffee and Prayers

Whether your "past" is many years ago, or your "past" is 24 hours ago, it doesn't matter. We are who HE says we are.

Who or what someone says we are or have done is of no consequence. If you are His, you are bought and paid for, and you are a child of the King.

God is with us. Who can stand against us? Have a great day everyone.

"'No weapon formed against you shall prosper, and every tongue which rises against you in judgment you shall condemn. This is the heritage of the servants of the Lord, and their righteousness is from Me, 'Says the Lord." Isaiah 54:17

Coffee and Prayers this Cloudy Friday Morning.

We watched a movie a couple of years ago that was really heart wrenching. "Extremely Loud and Incredibly Close".

It's about a 9 year old boy named Oskar Schell, whose dad (Tom Hanks) died in the attacks of 9-11. Oskar was very close to his dad. His dad tried to teach him to confront his fears. And he was afraid of nearly everything.

Oskar carries a dark secret about 9-11, the day he only refers to as 'The Worst Day'. His dad had called home several times that day and left messages on the answering machine. The last one he only kept repeating 'Are you there, are you there?'. Oskar only reveals to one other person that he had actually just got home from school and was listening to the voice of his father on the answering machine, but was terrified to answer.

He was listening to the voice of his father, and saw on live TV, the tower collapse where his father was trapped. He then collapses just as the towers collapsed.

Oskar replaces the answering machine with a new one and keeps hidden the machine with the calls from his father. He goes back and traces his steps from the calls that day and where he was a year after "the worst day". Oskar discovers a mysterious key in a vase in his father's closet. He discovers that it is a key to a safe deposit box, and the only clue is the word "Black" on the small brown envelope that held the key. He realizes that it obviously had something to do with someone named Black.

Coffee and Prayers

He obtains the names of all families named Black in the New York City area. He puts together an elaborate map and plan to visit every single Black family in the city. A plan that will take him 3 years. As he visits each family and explains about the key, none of whom have a clue about it, each family is touched by his story. They all except for one take him in, treat him with kindness, and they touch each other's lives in a small way.

It is later that Oskar discovers that the key had a connection to one of the first Blacks he contacted, Abby Black. The key had been hidden in a vase that belonged to her ex father in law and was sold to Oskar's dad at an estate sale by her ex-husband, who did not know the key was in the vase until he finally read a letter written to him by his late father.

When Oskar delivers the safe deposit key to William Black, he offers to share whatever it was in the box with Oskar, who refuses.

Angered by the turn of events, Oskar returns home and begins to destroy the elaborate maps and books and notes he had compiled. It was then that Oskar's mother (Sandra Bullock) steps in and reveals that she had figured out his plan, and had visited each family before Oskar did. She explained to them before-hand that her son would visit each one them and what he was seeking.

There is much more to the story, but it struck me that God does what Oskar's mom does at times. We may think that He is uninterested and is going on about His business and cares nothing about what we are doing or where we are going. Oskar's mom revealed that she had trailed him everywhere he went. She had kept an eye on him. She had paved a way for him and was very much involved even though he never knew it. Oskar had even at one point in the movie told his mom that he wished it had been her in the building that day instead of his dad. His mother simply said, "So do I".

We can be that way at times.

We can get angry with God and think that He is uninvolved with what is happening to us. We, as Oskar did in the movie, don't even realize that God is way ahead of us and paving the way in our circumstances.

Think on that as you go about your day. Even when we come across "roadblocks", they are, more times than not, put there by God to keep us safe and to detour us around something that we may want but

Coffee and Prayers

may not be good for us. Never think that God is not involved in our daily lives.

Have a great day everyone.

"He who dwells in the secret place of the Most High Shall abide under the shadow of the Almighty. I will say of the Lord, 'He is my refuge and my fortress;

My God, in Him I will trust.' Surely He shall deliver you from the snare of the fowler
And from the perilous pestilence.
He shall cover you with His feathers,
And under His wings you shall take refuge;
His truth shall be your shield and buckler.

You shall not be afraid of the terror by night,
Nor of the arrow that flies by day,
Nor of the pestilence that walks in darkness,
Nor of the destruction that lays waste at noonday."
Psalm 91: 1-6

Coffee and Prayers this Monday Morning.

More prayers than usual, as these days are trying times.

I saw on TV guide the other day, the movie titled "The Purge". There's even a sequel now I believe.

There's also a miniseries now.

I only watched part of the original movie. The plot of the movie is a United States in the not too distant future. One day a year, all laws are suspended, emergency services are suspended, and anyone can do anything within that 12-hour period that the "Purge" occurs. Everything is legal within that period, including murder.

So apparently, anyone can go and rob, steal, burn, or do whatever they want to do with absolutely no recourse and no consequences in this "world". That concept got me to thinking. What do you suppose would happen if this scenario were to actually ever become reality? Many of you are thinking, "That could never happen."

Really?

Consider for a moment all of the things in the Bible that God prohibits that are legal now, things that only a dozen or so years ago would be heard of. That is a conversation for later. Suppose however, that scenario were real here.

What do you think most people would do?

Would they take refuge in their homes, armed to defend themselves, their families and property? Would they take advantage of this period to go exact revenge upon those who have harmed or wronged them? Would they steal, kill, destroy, riot, murder, rape? It is sad to think, but I cannot help but believe that many would take advantage of it. After all, if it is legal, it is okay then, right? Would even Christians say, "It is legal, I can do it" and then go back to living under the law once the "Purge" is over? Is something being legal and even widespread accepted right? Absolutely not.

There were many things that were legal, even commanded in Biblical times, especially under pagan rulers, but that did not make it right in God's eyes.

We are to obey the law, as long as the law is just, as long as it does not contradict God's laws. In addition, just because something is legal under our laws, that does not mean that we have to accept it when it is against His laws. And we are subject to God first, not the government. Moreover, when our laws make obeying His laws ILLEGAL, we are still subject to HIM first.

Things are upside down in this world today. We have people who can on TV and call women such as Sarah Palin and Sarah Sanders every vile name in the book and call it "free speech". On the other side, we have government threatening us if we "offend" Muslims with our speech and suspending little children for even saying the word "gun."

We have abortion clinics where "doctors" have done and continue to murder not only infants in early trimesters of pregnancy of their mothers, they have murdered babies who are full term, breathing and crying babies. In addition, this nation for the most part yawns and shrugs its shoulders.

I could make a list of such other examples that could go on for dozens of pages, but you get my point. We have a changing culture here where good has become bad, right has become wrong, unmoral has become accepted. We are expected by society to not only go along with what is wrong, we are expected to EMBRACE it and celebrate it.

I can only say that it is a sign of the times. It is only going to get worse. We as Christians, however, know that there are many signs that it is getting close to our Homecoming. I wonder more often now more than ever when the Father will say to Christ, "Son, go and get My children."

It is easy to get discouraged when we merely look around. As my Pastor says, "Don't look around, look UP!" We have His promise, we have His Word, and we have His protection, His grace and His mercy.

This world may be losing its mind, but we do not have to lose our minds with it. This is just a temporary home for us. He is coming back and we will not have to endure the slings and arrows of this world much longer. Let us keep looking up, keep praying for one another, keep lifting one another up, keep praying for this nation, and never lose hope.

Have a great day everyone.

"For the Lord Himself will descend from Heaven with a shout, with the voice of an archangel, and with the trumpet of God. And the dead in Christ will rise first. Then we who are alive and remain shall be caught up together with them in the clouds to meet the Lord in the air. And thus we shall always be with the Lord." 1 Thessalonians 4:16-17

Coffee and Prayers

Coffee and Prayers this Cold Lord's Day.

The other day I was watching a video clip from "Back to The Future." As you may know, the movie is about a high school student named Marty McFly. His friend, an old scientist named Doc Brown invents a time machine, and Marty is accidentally sent back in time 30 years, from 1985 to 1955. Marty was in his home town, but he was in an era 30 years behind his.

I remember watching it at the movies back in '85 and thinking about how much life has changed since 1955. I realized that movie is 32 years old! How things have changed since then. What we considered "high tech" in 85 is antique now. The movie camera that Marty had, the Walkman, and so on.

It's amazing how many things become obsolete over the years. They become useless. Even the DeLorean car that was the time machine. Only a few of the DeLorean's were even made.

Years pass and objects become useless. They wear out, they lose their worth and value.

Even some in society now think that of humans. When they are born a certain way or when they reach a certain age, they are considered relics, useless.

No matter how life and time marches on, our value to God never diminishes. We never become obsolete to Him. We never will. We are the same to Him today as we were 30 years ago. That which we valued then may have changed, that which the world and society valued may have changed, but God hadn't changed His opinion or His mind. He puts our past behind, He placed our sins on the cross. He has our future, our life with Him forever in heaven in mind.

2017 has been hard on my family. I was in the hospital, Cindy was in the hospital, my mom was in the hospital, and I know several now who are currently in the hospital.

It doesn't matter what has happened, because God is still on His throne. He's still in charge.

The old year is done, the old years are done. What lies ahead, only God knows, but He DOES KNOW! Have a great day everyone. "'Do not remember the former things, Nor consider the things of old. Behold, I will do a new thing, Now it shall spring forth; Shall you not know it? I will even make a road in the wilderness, And rivers in the desert.'" Isaiah 43:18-19

Coffee and Prayers

Coffee and Prayers this Cold but Clear Thursday.

The weekend is barely visible, but will soon be here.

Several years ago when I was going to visit one of my daughters in her first apartment in Nashville. I had her address , but I'd never been to this apartment .Nashville has always been a confusing city to navigate in to me , but I had the address put into my GPS , and I was on my way that Saturday morning . The three and a half hour trip was without incident until I hit the outskirts of Nashville and my GPS shut off! I turned it back on, only to have it shut off after 30 seconds, time and time again. The cord was plugged into the power source on my dashboard. What in the world was going on with it? All I knew about her apartment was that it was "only 2 miles from Lispcomb", where she was going to school. Of course there are a thousand apartments within 2 miles of there.

I tried calling, only to have her phone go straight to voicemail. I checked the GPS cord once more. Only this time I discovered that it wasn't my GPS cord that was plugged in, it was my phone cord! I laughed at myself, plugged in my GPS, making SURE it truly was plugged in, and it led me right to her driveway.

Coffee and Prayers

I thought I had been plugged in all that time, only to discover that I'd been plugged in all wrong. I sincerely thought I was plugged in. But I was sincerely wrong.

Such is life sometimes. How many people are "plugged in" to the wrong source in life? How many rely upon that job to sustain them? How many rely upon that relationship, that retirement, that wealth to sustain them? How many rely upon horoscopes, psychics, or even some lifestyle? Maybe they simply rely upon themselves. They've done okay up until now, so why change? Like that GPS, maybe they made it 95% of the way. But it was that last 5% that mattered MOST. If it's a job or wealth you depend upon, what happens when that is suddenly gone? There were many, many people who took their own lives when the crash of 1929 occurred. They lost their wealth; therefore they lost their will to live because that was all they had. It's bad to lose a good job, I know from experience. But my job wasn't my provider. Jesus was and still is my provider. He saw me through. It's always tragic to lose a spouse, a parent, or child. If that relationship with that person or persons is the only thing that sustains a person, then what happens when that ends?

If we have CHRIST as our main source, we need not ever worry about that source ending. When He is ours, we are His, its forever. Literally. He won't take us 95% of the way and then leave.

What are you depending upon as your source? Sincerity about it doesn't matter. Sincerity doesn't equal truth. I can sincerely believe that I'm eating candy, but if it is truly rat poison, then I will die.

Being His means that when all else fails, He won't let you fall. He's the ONLY constant in a world that gets more insane every day. Make HIM your source. Have a great day everyone.

"Let your conduct be without covetousness; be content with such things as you have. For He Himself has said, 'I will never leave you nor forsake you.' So we may boldly say: 'The Lord is my helper; I will not fear. What can man do to me?'" Hebrews 13:5-6

Coffee and Prayers this Cold Wednesday Morning.

I watched an episode of "Blue Bloods" the other night that I was thinking about. The show centers around NYC Police Commissioner Frank Reagan and his family. His dad a retired NYC Police Officer and

Coffee and Prayers

Commissioner, and his sons who are NYPD and his daughter, a District Attorney.

In this episode, Reagan decides to visit some precincts on the midnight shift. He is trying to learn more about the
35,000 plus men and women who comprise the NYPD in this city of over ten million.

As he goes around that night, he suspects something is amiss when some of the officer's paperwork isn't what it should be, and each time he tries to get in touch with that precinct commander, he is mysteriously "out of pocket".

When the precinct commander calls in sick the next night, Reagan decides to go to his home, suspecting blatant misbehavior. He discovers the Lieutenant fully clothed and in good health. When Reagan confronts him, the Lieutenant shows him his wife, in a hospital bed right there in their home. The Lieutenant explains she is in her final few days, due to ALS (Lou Gehrig's Disease).

Reagan realizes that this man was so loved and respected by his officers under him that they risked their careers to cover for him so he could spend the last days of his wife's life with her. The episode ends with Reagan going into the "cop bar" where that precinct's police hung out after their tours.

Coffee and Prayers

Reagan tells them he is off duty as well and buys around for everyone. He has a greater respect for his officers and they have a greater respect for him. Such is life.

How many people are such great leaders that those he or she commands would risk their lives for them? Or careers? Or anything?

I've had some great people who have led me. Most of whom I'd have laid down all for. And it worked both ways. Those I've led and commanded, I've had a great mutual love and respect relationship.

How many people have a supervisor or other "leader" that they know they can go to for help, or counsel?

In leadership positions, you should try to know your people, their families, their hobbies, their interests. You should want to know what motivates them, what they care about.

If I've learned one thing in the army, it's this: TAKE CARE OF YOUR PEOPLE!

Respect works both ways, and it must be given to be received.

Coffee and Prayers

It's amazing to me, however, that our salvation is not like this. We can never be worthy, we can never earn it, we can never do enough "good" to be acceptable. The Lord took care of all that on the cross. We didn't have to earn anything or be respected. We have no way at all to do anything worthy of Jesus dying for us.

Those in law enforcement and the military know that each day may be the day they have to make that ultimate sacrifice. Not for just someone you love or respect, but for a total stranger.

Christ laid His life down for us all, and all anyone has to do is just accept Him and salvation is a done deal for us.

He loves us even when we aren't lovable.

We can't do anything that will make Him love us more. We cannot do anything to make Him love us less. The most vile of us, unwanted, unloved, unrespected, can gain salvation.
Christ doesn't measure by our standards.

Unlike Reagan in that episode, He knows the entire story of all of us from the very beginning.

He doesn't have to learn about us, he already knows.

Coffee and Prayers

Have a great day everyone.

"'Greater love has no one than this, than to lay down one's life for his friends.'" John 15:13

Coffee and Prayers this Cool Wednesday Morning.

The other night Cindy and I went to see "Heaven is for Real". It is based on the true story of the Burpo family. Todd Burpo is the pastor of a small church in a small Nebraska town. His wife Sonya assists him as a pastor's wife .They have a daughter, Cassie, 8, and a son, Colton, who is 4. Todd makes a living with his door company, as well as his small salary from the church, and is on the town's volunteer fire department. The town is supportive of one another, and when Colton falls ill with a ruptured appendix, he is near death in the hospital. The entire town stops and prays for Colton. Sonya is in the waiting room calling friends for prayer. Todd is in the hospital chapel, and is angry with God.

Colton survives, and when he awakens, he has changed somewhat. Sort of "matter-of-factly", he tells his dad about how he saw his mom in one room on the phone, he in another, yelling at God.

Coffee and Prayers

Todd is confounded as to how he would know this. As the story unfolds, Colton, when pressed, tells of how he went to heaven. He describes how beautiful it is, all the animals there and how young everyone is. He even tells how he met "Pop", Todd's grandpa, who had died when Todd was a child. When showed a picture of "Pop" as an old man, Colton says "No, that's not him." When showed a picture of Pop as a young man, Colton identifies him. Colton even describes how he met Jesus and sat on His lap!

The story spreads, and now the town begins to turn on the Burpo's. They are being laughed at and Todd is about to be removed from the church. The story is gaining attention. Negative attention. The Burpo's don't know what to do. Young Colton one day talks about his sister he didn't know about. When his Mom says "You know that Cassie is your sister." "No, not Cassie, my sister that died in your tummy. I met her in heaven." Sonya is floored. She had miscarried a baby before Cassie was born. They had never told anyone! How could he possibly have known this? I won't give any more about this true story away. It just really amazed me that those who professed to believe so much , who prayed with the Burpo's, would turn when confronted with the fact that Heaven is REAL. I suppose that I just don't understand why people would pay so much lip service to salvation, and yet don't truly believe in it.

Coffee and Prayers

Why would an innocent little 4 year old's experience in heaven scare some so much?

This was asked in the movie. So why is it that so many doubt? I can understand doubts about an adult who may could have an ulterior motive in claiming this. A 4 year old has no such ulterior motives .What concerns me is so many people who do the "church thing", does the "prayer thing", does all of the "outside" things that show that they are a Christian, yet do not truly believe what they profess to believe! The only analogy that I can think of is maybe Santa. People put out Santa's, tell their kids about him, prep their kids about him, set out cookies and milk for him, but know all along that he doesn't exist.

They do the same thing with Jesus. They do all the things connected with Him, but in their hearts don't truly believe anything about Him as being real. We, as true believers KNOW that He, Jesus, is real. We know He's alive. We know He helps us daily. He's not a "Santa" to us. I had nowhere near the experience that the real Colton had, but I HAVE been dead. I WAS brought back. I know what I saw. I know what I experienced. I know what I felt. I know what it is like to be on the other side, if only for brief moment.

Coffee and Prayers

Where are your beliefs? Is Christ merely a "Santa" to you? Do you profess Him as a cultural thing only? Do you profess Him as a social thing only? Or do you know Him personally? Is He your Savior? Is He truly? Has He placed His hands on you in your darkest moments? Has He spoken words of comfort to you when you were at your lowest? Has He heard your screams in the darkness? Do you know Him?

I'm not asking if you know ABOUT Him, I'm asking if you KNOW HIM. Is He your Savior or merely a symbol of a social "norm" that you're expected to have? When confronted about the reality of a Savior and a place where His people will dwell with Him for all eternity, are you comforted? Or does it scare you to death? If it scares you, then it's time to examine your faith and turn it over to Him. Give Him your life. Trust in Him.

My friends, please believe me, Heaven is for real.

If we are His, truly His, it's there waiting for us. Have a great day everyone. "'Let not your heart be troubled; you believe in God, believe also in Me. In My Father's house are many mansions; if it were not so, I would have told you. I go to prepare a place for you. And if I go and prepare a place for you, I will come again and receive you to Myself; that where I am, there you may be also. And where

I go you know, and the way you know.'" John 14:1-4

Coffee and Prayers this cool Morning.

I wanted to repost this from a couple of years ago. Hope it helps at least one person today.

I was thinking this morning about an incident that happened a few years ago. I was somewhere in Memphis and I noticed this older gentleman's cap. There was an emblem on it, no words. I recognized it and asked him "Are you RCMP?" (Royal Canadian Mounted Police) His face broke out in a smile as he reached out to shake my hand. He said "I've been here with my wife on holiday for over a week now, and you are the first American who knew what this was. Everyone else thinks it is the Crown Royal Whiskey emblem!"

He was a retired RCMP officer.

He wore the emblem of his profession proudly, and yet no one else knew what it was. He and his wife were very nice, and they talked to me for a few minutes there as if they'd known me forever. This was a proud Canadian who had served his country and the public for many years. He felt disrespected because no one respected the symbol of authority that he wore.

A lot of people will look at our "symbols". They will wrongly judge what we are about. They will see a lack of a symbol and think wrongly.

You drive a truck? Must be a redneck!

A success in business? Must've cheated people to get to the top! A successful woman? She couldn't have possibly made it on her own!

A jock? He's dumb. A blonde? She's ditzy!

A soldier? Uneducated!

A Christian? Hypocrite! Bible thumper!

God sees us as who we TRULY are. He recognizes all that we are. He never mistakes our outward "symbols" as something less, nor as of something more.

No matter what society "labels" us, when we are His, we are His. People saw that man's cap and assumed that he was a Crown Royal drinker. Did that change ANYTHING about him? Absolutely not.

Coffee and Prayers

His service was not changed one bit by a single person.

Our "reputation" is what people assume about us. Our character is what God KNOWS about us. Nothing is hidden from Him, good or bad.

We aren't the sum of our actions, we are the sum of His mercy and grace, and His sacrifice on the cross for us .People will tell others lies about us. They will give false reports about us to others. And many will believe simply on someone else's word.

There is really nothing that we can do about that. All we can do is just live our lives the best we can and let God handle it. When people spread false rumors and bring false reports of someone else's "evil", they often bring a curse upon themselves.

God sees us, He knows us.

We are who He says we are, not who gossipers assume we are.

Have a great day everyone.

"For I hear the slander of many; Fear is on every side; While they take counsel together against me, They scheme to take away my life. But as for me, I trust in You, O Lord; I say, "You are my God." My times are in Your hand; Deliver me from the hand of my enemies, And from those who persecute me. Make Your face shine upon Your servant; Save me for Your mercies' sake. Do not let me be ashamed, O Lord, for I have called upon You; Let the wicked be ashamed; Let them be silent in the grave. Let the lying lips be put to silence, Which speak insolent things proudly and contemptuously against the righteous." Psalm 31:13-18

Coffee and Prayers this Pleasant Friday Morning.

Looking forward to my first holiday off since Thanksgiving.

I recently read a friend's post in which she was telling of her first job. The owner was a man in his 70's, a self-made millionaire. Gruff spoken, she was intimidated by him. She had to stop him one day as he was leaving to ask him something. She said she kept apologizing for taking up his time. She said he told her that there was no need to apologize, and that if he didn't take time to listen to those taking care of his business, he'd HAVE no business. He then told her that his time was no more valuable than hers. What's more, she even discovered that he had a lot of hearing loss which made him sound gruff.

She had been afraid of him for no reason.

I was watching a TV show that features some of the WWE wrestlers and their personal lives. Wrestler John Cena is in a relationship with Nikki Bella. She had been suspicious of his behavior of late. On his phone suspiciously, on his laptop suspiciously. He'd even said he was in the gym one day, and Nikki and her twin sister Brie ride by the gym, no John.

She was heartbroken at this shady behavior. When John confessed, it was a confession that he had been seeing a real estate agent. To buy Nikki a house that she had been talking about was her dream home. He had wanted to surprise her with buying her the home of her dreams.

I was once accused of trying to take over our little country church down in Carroll County, and was even called a "dictator "by a man who had not even been a member in decades. I told him I had no desire to "take over", and that all I had said and done was said and done in the open and if he ever bothered to come to church there he'd hear the truth.

Coffee and Prayers

Fear. Suspicion. The enemy, Satan, plants these seeds in our minds.

Jesus was accused by the Pharisee. He was looked upon with suspicion and eventually crucified.

This happens when we don't recognize the enemy. The REAL enemy. Satan is an expert at "drive-bys". Like a gangbanger, just drive by bad throw out a few shots. It doesn't matter who it hits, what lives it destroys.

We can't let unfounded thoughts or suspicions cloud our minds. We can't just stand there and let Satan do his drive by damage.

My friend settled the issue with her boss. She had no reason to fear him again. Nikki Bella learned her boyfriend was working to make her dreams come true. He wasn't cheating on her.

Jesus wasn't trying to destroy anything but the devil and that lifestyle that had so perverted God's laws.

Are we identifying the true enemy? The enemy is Satan, not those around us.

He not only drives by and fires at us, he also scatters his seeds of doubt, suspicion, discord, and so on. Then here lies on us to water them and keep them growing, as human nature will do when we don't know someone's heart. Remember who the enemy is. It's not that person always. Many times it's just the devil hoping his drive by shots hit and kill something. He hopes his seeds are cultivated by us enough to grow tall and thick enough to choke out our flowers of faith, hope, and love. Know who the enemy truly is, and don't give him any help.

He's already powerful enough.

Be a prayer warrior. Stay on your face before God. Ask Him to destroy the enemy. Don't try to do it alone. We all have enough working against us; let's don't work against one another.

Have a great day everyone.

"Then I sent to him, saying, 'No such things as you say are being done, but you invent them in your own heart.'" Nehemiah 6:8

Coffee and Prayers this Cold and Rainy Lord's Day.

Such a pretty day yesterday, and now it's pouring rain again. I wanted to repost the following that I had posted a while back.

Coffee and Prayers

I was thinking about the movie "Pearl Harbor". Before the attack, there was an effort in the Pacific to prepare for an emanate attack by the Japanese. Some thought that anchoring the entire fleet at Pearl was the best action. I remember the words of Admiral Husband E. Kimmel, the Commander in Chief of the Pacific Fleet. Admiral Kimmel said," A smart enemy hits you where you think you're safe." This is so true in life, not just in war. It happens with the criminal element all of the time. For most people, home is where they feel the safest. Yet a determined criminal will break in, and hit suddenly.

Most people feel safe at church, but criminals know that a parking lot full of cars represents an opportunity to hit, especially if he thinks they will be inside for at least an hour. Also the church goers are a target. Church isn't sacred to evil people. It's why many churches have security forces these days.

So what about spiritual attacks? Is Satan a smart enemy? You better believe he is.

Does he know where to hit you? Of course he does.

A poll conducted several years ago among Christian's states that most family squabbles happened in the hour or two before church on Sunday mornings. A sound tactic by the enemy.

Coffee and Prayers

Imagine a family rushing to get dressed for Sunday services. The kids mess up their church clothes, the mom is mad at the dad for not keeping an eye on them while she's getting ready, they go to get in the car and it has a flat, and now the dad is mad at the mom because he's been on her all week to take the car to get that slow leak fixed since he's been working late every day. The kids have been fussed at, so they're upset, the dad has been fussed at so he's upset, the mom has been fussed at so she's upset.

The entire family is in church and perhaps their hearts aren't on worship. They are all thinking about how mad or hurt they are now. Now this morning's worship is not about God, it's just an "I'm here, I showed up" experience. We (myself included and especially), often place the blame on that person instead of the enemy. We don't recognize that the enemy has a "divide and conquer" attitude. He hates for God to be worshipped. He hates to see God glorified .So what is the best defense? PRAY! Easy to say, hard to do. When we get mad at that spouse or boyfriend or girlfriend or child or whoever, we want to KEEP that "mad". We don't want to praise God and ask Him to calm us, to give us peace, or to bless that person. We want to say "I'm right in this."

Well we may BE right.

Coffee and Prayers

There is nothing wrong with getting angry. We wouldn't be human if we didn't. We have to learn to RESPOND, rather than to REACT. Easy to say, hard to do. We must remember that when we get angry at a spouse or whoever, it is the enemy who is THE ENEMY. Being angry at someone doesn't make them the enemy. Sometimes we just need to walk away for an hour or so and think about it and pray about it. Maybe think about when maybe we have made someone else angry, or hurt them. Did WE do it intentionally? Or were WE misunderstood?

We face a smart enemy in Satan. He's not omniscient nor omnipresent as God is, but he has his minions, his demons, those fallen angels who followed him when he was cast out of heaven. They roam the earth looking for "safe" places to attack us.

Remember who the enemy is. And remember that God is more powerful. Pray without ceasing! Pray for those you are angry with. Pray for your own peace. When the enemy pits us against one another and distracts us from worship and praise and prayer, he wins a little battle. Take heart.

Those of us who have read the final chapter know that we win.

Coffee and Prayers

Have a good day everyone.

"For we do not wrestle against flesh and blood, but against principalities, against powers, against the rulers of the darkness of this age, against spiritual hosts of wickedness in the heavenly places." Ephesians 6:126

Coffee and Prayers on the Deck this Cool Monday Morning.

I was thinking about a story that I've posted before, but I feel compelled to post it again, that perhaps someone may need it this morning.

When I was about 12 years old, we were given a border collie named "Gal". Her owners had abused her, especially the man in the family. She was unwanted by them and unloved. For all 3 years of her life she'd been abused and neglected.

When they brought her to our house and put her in the back yard, she immediately ran into the dog house in the back of the yard.

I tried coaxing her out, but she remained cowered in the back of the dog house, eyes wide with fear.

Coffee and Prayers

I set water and food outside of her house. For a couple of days she was too scared to even stick her head out to eat.

Each day when I would go out, she was still in the dog house. I spoke gently and kind to her. I told her she was safe, and tried and tried to coax her out.

She would eventually stick her head out when I would leave and eat a bite and drink her water. The sound of the back door opening would send her back to the rear of her house.

I began to get discouraged at her fear of me. I felt rejected. I only wanted to love her and be loved in return. Her past hurts, however, still haunted her and she trusted no one.

Some dogs will bite out of fear. She, however, never tried to bite.

I was hurt at her rejection of me.

I had done nothing to hurt her, yet I felt she was punishing me by her rejection of me.

Why was she rejecting me? I had done her no harm and meant her no harm.

Coffee and Prayers

Over the days, I would notice that she would eventually venture out after I set her food out and went back inside. She would carefully smell around where I had been.

Opening the door would send her running into her house again.

I eventually accepted the fact that she may never accept me, never love me. I was about to tell my Mom that I didn't want her any longer.

I didn't give up on her though. I kept putting her food out. I would then just stay in the back yard and keep my distance.

She would leerily look my way and venture out, never looking away from me. As time went by, she did eventually one day, carefully sniff my hand one day as she still kept in the safety of her doghouse.

She eventually after that let me touch her, oh so carefully. I would speak to her softly and gently. I would tell her "It's okay Gal, it's okay."

As I would carefully pet her head, her body still safely in her house, her eyes seemed to say "Please don't hurt me."

Coffee and Prayers

One day, she finally came out and I carefully petted her. She was still afraid, yet there was progress.

As time went by, she was no longer afraid. The sound of the door opening no longer sent her running away; it sent her running towards me. She wagged her tail and leaned against me as I hugged her. Her eyes no longer were wide with fear. They no longer seemed to say "Please don't hurt me." Now her eyes seemed to say "Thank you for loving me."

We had her for several years until she died. She was a sweet dog who deserved so much better than what was done to her.

She was so scarred, emotionally, she could have never healed.

My patience with her paid off. It wasn't overnight, it wasn't immediate. It was a long and arduous process.

There are so many people who are just like that. They withdraw into themselves due to past hurts and abuse or neglect.

Each and every hurt that we have, be we that bad or not, adds up in our lives.

Coffee and Prayers

We can sometimes just decide that it's best just to stay safe in our emotional dog house rather than to face the possibility of one more hurt.

Fortunately Jesus understands this. He carefully and patiently feeds us emotionally and spiritually when we are open to Him.

He will allow people into our lives who will give us Godly and Biblical counsel, pray for us, pray with us, love us, hold us, and be there for us through it all.

It can take a lot of prayer, and a lot of seeking His face in His will for us in trying to heal. We can be healed; we can intervene with prayer for others to be healed. We cannot change anyone or heal them on our own, nor can they on their own.

God, however, can bring that spark to the eyes of the hurt. They will no longer be wide with fear, nor any longer seem to say "Please don't hurt me." They will say "Thank You for loving me."

Have a great day everyone.

"He heals the brokenhearted
And binds up their wounds." Psalm 147:3

Coffee and Prayers

Coffee and Prayers this Lord's Day.

Looking forward to being in the Lord's house this morning to worship with other believers.

Several years ago, I heard of a church in another town. It was a fairly large church. Several members had reached out into one of the poorest neighborhoods, and had convinced some of the teen boys and girls to come to church, and become involved in the youth program.

After a couple of weeks, some others in the church got these kids together and told them that if they were going to be coming to church there, the boys needed to be wearing shirts and ties, and the girls should be wearing dresses. Now these were very poor kids. And needless to say, they left to never come back. It broke my heart when I heard that. That was over 15 years ago. I wonder if any of them ever set foot in a church again.

I once had a man tell me that his job was to stand at the door of their church and turn away anyone who wasn't dressed up. I asked, "What if some man who was dirty, unshaven, wearing ragged clothes and all came up, would you turn him away?" "Yes, I'd tell him he can't come in!" he replied. "Well, I was just describing John the Baptist" I told him.

Coffee and Prayers

I once heard the testimony of a woman who, after her shift as a cocktail waitress at a local casino, decided to go to church. She didn't have time to change clothes. She said that she was afraid that she'd be turned away in her cocktail waitress dress. She said that she was welcomed, smiled at, and made to feel at home.

As I sit here this morning, I'm dismayed by so much that is going on in the world. So much that is backwards, upside down, right that is being called wrong, wrong that is being called right, and so on.

I think above all what is disturbing above all else is how we as Christians sometimes tend to want to think of Christianity as an exclusive "club". We don't want "those people" getting saved. We don't want "his kind" or "her kind" in "our church."

Didn't you hear? He lost his job! Didn't you hear? She is divorced! Didn't you hear? Their teenager is on drugs!

Didn't you hear? Their teenage daughter is pregnant! Didn't you hear? They are sinners! They do this, or they do that, whatever the case may be. We don't like how they dress, we don't like how they look. We don't "need" any more people in this church! Ever hear Christians with the attitude? And God forbid a visitor sit in "their spot"!

Coffee and Prayers

I've visited churches where I've had people look at me as if I were a wet dog at an outdoor wedding. No smiles, no welcome. Only looks.

It's no wonder that so many people are put off by so many church going people. God doesn't assign seats in church. Do you really think that you are doing the Lord's work by rejecting that stranger in HIS house? Who did Jesus reject by appearance, income, clothing, background, etc? Can you name anyone?

Jesus' harshest judgement was towards those who had that "I'm Godly and I'm better than you" attitude. Those who had turned their backs on God long ago and sat in judgement of others based on what THEY thought was "right", not what is Biblical.

I've heard people say "I don't want_____in MY church." YOUR church?

To me, the more people who are in true, Bible believing and preaching churches, the more who will hear the word and experience salvation.

When I hear of someone saying that they don't want so and so going to "their church", it saddens me to no end. I WANT the sinners coming to church. (without them, every single church would be completely empty). I WANT those who have a warped sense of God, His word, His grace, to HEAR His word. I WANT people who think that church is just a "cultural" thing to experience being in the presence of the Holy Spirit. I want those what have warped sense of God and His word to hear the true word.

I don't care what color or creed or national origin anyone is. If they are worshiping our God, they are my brother, my sister.

And yes I have been guilty of passing MY judgement on others when I don't know their story nor their struggles. There isn't a day that goes by that I'm not thankful that He died to pay for my hypocrisy, my attitude, my oversight, my shortsightedness, and all of the other sins of which I'm guilty.

I thank Him that it's been paid for on the cross. And I pray each day that I overcome that which I need to overcome, and I surrender to that which I need to surrender to.

Have a great day everyone.

"As Jesus passed on from there, He saw a man named Matthew sitting at the tax office. And He said to him, 'Follow Me.' So he arose and followed Him. Now it happened, as Jesus sat at the table in the house, that behold, many tax collectors and sinners same and sat down with Him and His disciples. And when the Pharisees saw it, they said to His disciples, 'Why does your Teacher eat with tax collectors and sinner?' When Jesus heard that, He said to them, 'Those who are well have no need of physician, but those who are sick. But go and learn what this means: "I desire mercy and not sacrifice.' For I did not come to call the righteous, but sinners, to repentance.'" Matthew 9:9-13

Coffee and Prayers this Rainy Saturday Morning.

I was getting the last of some tea out of a large decanter Saturday, I thought about something that happened at drill years ago.

One morning Colonel Cole, the Chief of Staff, was paying a visit to our unit. (The Chief of Staff is the "right-hand man" to the Adjutant General). Colonel Cole was a super nice guy. He looked the part of a Colonel, and in fact looked just like "central casting" had picked him for the part.

We had a large 30 cup coffee urn, and Colonel Cole was trying to get a cup of coffee, the last cup, from the urn. He was tilting the urn towards himself, trying to turn the spout and hold the cup. He glanced over at one of our men, a little sergeant named Larkins. Now Larkins was a good guy, a good soldier, extremely introverted and quiet. He stood there, arms folded, just watching Colonel Cole struggle. Colonel Cole glanced at Larkins and asked "Well am I going to have to hold my cup, tilt the pot and hold open the spigot all at the same time?" Without a second's9/28/21, hesitation, Larkins replied "That's the way I had to do it sir", and walked off! As several of us had to walk off, about to bust a gut laughing, our Sergeant Major jumped into action to help the Colonel.

Life can be like that at times, and of course much more complicated than a cup of coffee. We have struggles and it seems that everyone else is just standing around watching, just happy that it's not them.

How do we help others when it seems that we are helpless to do so? All that we can do at times is just let them know we are there, are praying for them, and that they aren't alone. Life is full of mountains and valleys. And many time sit seems like we are going through those valleys alone. And when we get to the mountain top we want to forget about those in their valleys. Maybe we can jump in and lend a hand. Maybe we can only pray for that person, that family in their situation. Their son is addicted? Do we just thank the Lord it isn't our son? Or do we sit in judgment? Their teen daughter is pregnant? What do we do for them? Judge and thank God it's not OUR daughter, or lift them up in prayers? We see someone lose their job, are we thankful it's not us, or do we pray for them and do all we can for them? It's easy to just stand there, knowing we've "had our coffee", and just watch others struggle. We have to take our blinders off to what others are going through.

I wish that I was guiltless in this, but it's very easy to get distracted by our own lives and forget the struggles of others. I certainly need to improve in this and will pray that God opens my eyes in this. We will all struggle at some point.

But we should pray with and for others, be glad for them when they achieve something, and be sympathetic and empathetic to everyone. I know that I've been prayed for when I struggled in every area of life. And I will make a concerted effort to do the same for others.

By the same token, we should not be envious of those who seem to have it "all together." We don't know what they struggle with or against.

Coffee and Prayers

Let's all lift one another up, let's pray for one another. Let's stay strong and keep the faith. Have a great day everyone.

"Let love be without hypocrisy. Abhor what is evil. Cling to what is good. Be kindly affectionate to one another with brotherly love, in honor giving preference to one another; not lagging in diligence, fervent in spirit, serving the Lord; rejoicing in hope, patient in tribulation, continuing steadfastly in prayer; distributing to the needs of the saints, given to hospitality. Bless those who persecute you; bless and do not curse. Rejoice with those who rejoice, and weep with those who weep. Be of the same mind toward one another. Do not set your mind on high things, but associate with the humble. Do not be wise in your own opinion. Repay no one evil for evil. Have regard for good things in the sight of all men. If it is possible, as much as depends on you, live peaceably with all men. Beloved, do not avenge yourselves, but rather give place to wrath; for it is written, "Vengeance is Mine, I will repay," says the Lord. Therefore "If your enemy is hungry, feed him; If he is thirsty, give him a drink; For in so doing you will heap coals of fire on his head." Do not be overcome by evil, but overcome evil with good." Romans 12:9-21

Coffee and Prayers

Coffee and Prayers this Lord's Day.

This morning, we will do as millions around the world will. We will gather with our fellow believers in our churches across the world.

After a long week of running wide open, 12 hour work days, and stresses beyond comprehension, today I will slowdown and worship Him in His House. He's been with me since my birth, He's with me daily.

A friend of mine made a point about Memorial Day on his post. It's the exact same thing I'd been thinking. And have been thinking for years. This is Memorial Day weekend. A day set aside to HONOR those who have died in combat for this nation. Turn on the radio or TV, open a newspaper. You will be inundated with "Memorial Day sales." Car dealerships. Clothing stores. JC Penny seems to always have a "white sale". And for some odd reason, a lot of mattress sales. This is how we "honor" our war dead, with sales?

Of course we do the same with Independence Day. The day we celebrate our nation's birth. It's a day to celebrate, yes, but with sales?

Coffee and Prayers

Then there is Thanksgiving. A day set aside to give thanks to God for all our blessings. (Something we should do daily). We are inundated with "sales".

Then there is Christmas. The day we celebrate the birth of Christ. The "sales" pitch for Christmas begins really in August. It's called the "giving season". Meaning giving gifts that you've spent money on. Meaning appealing to spending money and making money. It's not truly about "giving", it's about spending.

We honor our war dead with an appeal to us to spend money. We honor our nation's birth with an appeal to make money. We honor a day of thanks with an appeal to make money. And we honor our Savior's birth (and to a lesser degree, His crucifixion and resurrection) with appeals to make money. And when I say make money, I mean for these companies to make money. It's an appeal to us to "save" money by spending more of it.

It's sad, but it's the world we live in. Let's not dishonor our war dead by joining this mentality. Let's not dishonor our Lord by participating in a spending spree that is supposedly for Him.

Let's not join those who place the "almighty dollar" above the Almighty God. Have a great day everyone.

"For the love of money is a root of all kinds of evil, for which some have strayed from the faith in their greediness, and pierced themselves through with many sorrows." 1 Timothy 6:10

Coffee and Prayers this Saturday Morning.

I was thinking about a book I read several years ago. I think it was titled "Cop Hunter." It was written by an NYC police officer named Vincent Murano, who went deep undercover to infiltrate the mob in NYC in the late '50s to expose corrupt cops inside the NYC police department. He was several years inside the mob and was instrumental in the arrest and conviction of several key mob figures, as well as many police officers.

Something that caught my attention and that has always stuck in my memory was how they, the mob, viewed him after it was discovered who he actually was. The mob would kill any of their own who turned on them. However, he said in his book that when their ranks were infiltrated as he did, they considered it almost "honorable," and that they respected anyone just doing their duty and their job. They would never attempt to harm his family because of even the harm that he did to their "business."

In the '60s however, when he began investigating the Jamaican drug mobs, things were different. Wives and children of these gang's enemies were fair game to these gangs. The world had changed in less than a decade. Changed for the worse. It's amazing how much the world has changed since the time I was a child. And not for the better. As my generation grew up, we always played cowboys, war, like we knights or kings, and so forth. There was always "good vs evil." I see how the world is now. How the line between "good and evil" has been blurred.

Our children's innocence is not lost, it is stolen by a world where sin is rampant. Those children whose spirits are gentle and kind, who have a love for their friends and family, who have respect for their parents, respect for authority, and the desire to serve God are constantly under attack. They are ridiculed. They have their self-esteem crushed. We see kids now who no longer emulate and respect those heroes and heroines. They instead want to be like those who are the most cynical and evil. They choose to be those who take and never give back. They disrespect their parents, they disrespect their elders, they disrespect the figures of authority such as the police, teachers, etc. They expect to be given and given, they take and they take, and they have no regard for anyone but themselves. They want to "shock" those around them. In the gym once I saw a teenage boy who had on a shirt with a credit card on the front.

I cannot put what words the caption in his shirt had, but it said that a body part of his was accepted everywhere. I once saw a teen downtown wearing a shirt that read "American by birth, Anti-Christ by choice." Was I shocked? YES, even after all that I have seen in my life. When we see, however, children who are NOT corrupted by this world, who respect their parents, who respect their elders, who respect their teachers, police, and so forth, it's like a breath of fresh air. It's hard not to get frustrated. It's hard to think that this world is going to hell on a freight train.

We see very few positive things on the news these days. It seems that we sometimes have our fingers in a leaking hole and the rest of the dam is crumbling around us. We just have to remember one thing. This is NOT going unnoticed by God. He is STILL God. He is bigger than what is going on in the world. Sometimes it seems that we are as Moses and the children of Israel. We have the sea to our backs and the enemy bearing down on us. We are as David sometimes. We are a young boy going out on a field of battle to face a ten-foot-tall,

500-pound giant who entire armies fear. We just have to hold on to our faith and know that God will open the sea for us, and close it on our pursuing enemies. We may be armed with just a few smooth stones, but God will strengthen us to sling a stone right into the skulls of the giants that we face.

The world is getting worse. But God hasn't changed. When your back is to the sea, know that God is still God. When the giant is telling you that he will feed the carcass to the birds, just remember. God is bigger. God is bigger. God is bigger. It's hard not to let fear crush your faith. Hold on tight and get ready to cross onto dry land. Be ready to cut the head off a giant when he falls dead in front of you. Let's keep one another prayed up everyone. Let's not forget that we are all in this together. The world has changed, but God hasn't and neither have we.

Have a great day everyone.

"Woe to them that call evil good, and good evil; that put darkness out for light, and light for darkness; that put bitter for sweet, and sweet for bitter!" Isaiah 5:20

Coffee and Prayers

Coffee and Prayers, and a Beautiful Dawning Day Arising.

I was thinking about how 34 years ago today I woke up for the first time at Ft McClellan, Alabama. I had arrived the day before, bewildered at my first day in the army. Life was different for me now. As people from all walks of life were experiencing this same thing, we were all realizing that this life was totally different from anything I'd imagined.

Today would be the day that all of us would have our heads shaved, uniforms issued. By noon, we all looked more alike. All of us were now hairless, and all of us were in OD Green fatigues. For the coming months, we would all share the same experience. All "individuality" was stripped away. We would now be working as a team. We would be broken down, frustrated, exhausted, confused. We learned to use our strengths to help others who were weak in those areas. We would correct one another.

We would learn from our Drill Sergeants very quickly what we were doing wrong or right. We would learn that we

RAN when we went somewhere. We learned that when told to do something, do it immediately! Quickly! We learned that when a Drill Sergeant came and put the brim of his hat against your head,

Coffee and Prayers

you were in deep trouble. You were about to be screamed at from the depths of hell it seemed. We were rushed through chow; eat it in 5 minutes, no time to taste it. Hurry to the next location, and wait. As the weeks went by, we became stronger. The 2 mile runs seemed like nothing. The push-ups were now easy. We all were becoming soldiers. We all were working as a team, a unit. We were brothers. We were concerned with how we performed as a platoon, not as individuals. We helped one another.

It can be this way in life. We can wake up one morning and feel as if we are in a new world. All that we have known life to be has been turned upside down.

In basic combat training we were broken down, then built up stronger. We were soldiers. If we are living life at all, we will be broken down at times. We will be stripped down. It's at these times that we need other believers there beside us. We need others praying for us. We need others lifting us up. We need help in our weakness from those who are stronger.

We need to all succeed as a believers, all of us. Let's concern ourselves with lifting all those up who are around us. We won't "graduate" from life until God calls us home.

Until then, we are ALWAYS "training". Have a great day everyone.

"Where do wars and fights come from among you? Do they not come from your desires for pleasure that war in your members? Is anyone among you suffering? Let him pray. Is anyone cheerful? Let him sing psalms. Is anyone among you sick? Let him call for the elders of the church, and let them pray over him, anointing him with oil in the name of the Lord. And the prayer of faith will save the sick, and the Lord will raise him up. And if he has committed sins, he will be forgiven. Confess your trespasses to one another, and pray for one another, that you may be healed. The effective, fervent prayer of a righteous man avails much. Elijah was a man with a nature like ours, and he prayed earnestly that it would not rain; and it did not rain on the land for three years and six months. And he prayed again, and the heaven gave rain, and the earth produced its fruit. Brethren, if anyone among you wanders from the truth, and someone turns him back, let him know that he who turns a sinner from the error of his way will save a soul from death and cover a multitude of sins." James 5:13-20

Coffee and Prayers

Coffee and Prayers this Thursday Morning.

A stomach bug had me flat on my back for two days. I haven't been sick in many moons, just hoping to get back to 100%.

I'm reposting this from a few years ago, hoping someone may need it today.

I was thinking last night about one of my favorite movies, "The Ten Commandments". Moses, when he had discovered that he had Hebrew parents, decided to disguise himself as a slave and join his brethren in the mud pits where bricks were made. Neither the slaves nor the Egyptian overseers recognized him as a Prince of Egypt.

He was also Commander of the Royal Army. He was Prince of Memphis, First Friend to the Pharaoh. He was bestowed with many titles and honors. He took his orders directly from Pharaoh. He answered to no one else on earth. Yet here he was in the mud pit with his Hebrew brethren, posing as a slave.

It was however Nefretiri, the Princess who was in love with Moses who recognized him. She had the guards bring him to her under the guise of needing another rower for her barge. When he was brought in to her, she mockingly asked "Do you not kneel before the Princess?' Moses, standing there before her, covered with mud replied "The mud has stiffened my knees..." Nefritiri then said "Shall I summon the guards?" To which Moses replied "Do you think THEY can bend them?"

It has always been one of my favorite scenes. Moses was seeking. He was seeing the injustice. He was seeing the misery. He was seeing the pain. He was seeing the death and the hopelessness. He placed himself actually in danger.

Moses even killed an Egyptian who was beating a Hebrew. The writings of Josephus and Phylo tell us that he killed the master builder Bacca to save Joshua.

While at that point, Moses had no idea that he had been guided by the hand of God his entire life. He had no idea that God had protected him from birth. He had been raised in and around the man-made 'gods' that the Egyptians worshiped.

Although he knew nothing of the true living God at that point, his strength, his courage, and all that compelled him to leave the luxury of royalty and take his place with his own people was in fact, guided by the God he didn't know.

Coffee and Prayers

We all know the rest of history as it pertains to this. Banished from Egypt, a shepherd for 40 years, and then he met God in the form of a burning bush and then a return to Egypt at God's hand to free the children of Israel.

Even when we were at points in our lives when we didn't know it, God was with us. God was guiding us. God was leading us. Even after many years of perhaps living a life of obscurity, God is preparing us for something.

Our strength to stand up for what is right, our courage to do what is right, our faith to know God will lead us in what

is right all come from God. Even for those who may just now be "seeking" God, He is guiding you at this point. He will reveal His plan for you, and He will see you through it. It may even require leaving a life that you have always known and living a simpler life with a true God, and not many false gods. Moses chose the living God, and has spent many thousands of years since his death in the arms of our Father. To have chosen the riches and luxuries of the false gods of Egypt would mean he would have spent many thousands of years in the torment of hell, separated from God forever.

Know that even when you are persecuted, even when you are knocked down there are those who would threaten to bend your knees towards something dangerous, God is there to give you the courage and strength and faith to know that they cannot bend them against your will. Have a great day everyone!

"By faith Moses, when he became of age, refused to be called the son of Pharaoh's daughter, choosing rather to suffer affliction with the people of God than to enjoy the passing pleasures of sin, esteeming the reproach of Christ greater riches than the treasures in Egypt; for he looked to the reward." Hebrews 11:24-26

Coffee and Prayers this Lord's Day.

Most people my age remember the old television show "The Lawrence Welk Show." It was very popular during the 60's and 70's. Each show had a theme, and musical performances in that theme. For example, they may pay tribute to a certain composer, songwriter, performer, or genre of music.

Coffee and Prayers

In 1971, one show was a tribute to Spiritual and Gospel music. And one song that was performed by Gail and Dale was a then fairly new song titled "One Toke Over the Line." It's still on YouTube, so it's not an urban myth. I actually viewed it.

Now the song begins "One toke over the line, sweet Jesus..." The song was absolutely NOT a "spiritual "song. Yes, it mentions Jesus, but not in a worshipful or reverent way. The song is about smoking pot. That segment was most likely done out of an extreme naivety. Not likely intentionally.

Some people can just see something with "Jesus" in it and believe it.

Just the other day, I saw a post where someone posted that Jesus was for free childcare, free food, free education, free healthcare, and was soft on crime. Since He had the children not be hindered from coming to Him, He was for "free childcare." Since He fed the multitudes, He was for

"free food." Since He taught, "free education." Since He healed, "free healthcare." And since He forgave a thief on the cross, soft on crime. Of course all of this was mentioned out of context, and of course for the purpose of pushing his own agenda. No mention of how Jesus taught that there must be confession and repentance, and acceptance of HIM. And He didn't forgive the OTHER THIEF on the cross because there was no repentance by him. No mention that He healed those who believed in Him. He fed those who came to Him. He didn't open a daycare center, He forbade us from hindering children from coming to Him. He forbade abuse of children.

Satan misquoted God's Word to Eve. He came to Jesus after His 40 days in the wilderness without food and tried to have Jesus feed Himself by turning stones into bread. He tried three times to have Jesus do what he said by quoting scripture. Out of context and to suit his own agenda of course.

Just because someone is quoting (and misquoting) The Bible, it doesn't mean that they are trying to preach the Word. It could be that they are pushing their own agenda.

And just because something SOUNDS Biblical, it doesn't mean that it IS Biblical.

There are many Biblical warnings of this in the Bible. Paul warns us in Romans 16:17-18, "Now I urge you, brethren, note those who cause divisions and offenses, contrary to the doctrine which you learned, and avoid them. For those who are such do not serve our Lord Jesus Christ, but their own belly, and by smooth words and flattering speech deceive the hearts of the simple."

Also in Jeremiah 14:14 "And the Lord said to me, 'The prophets prophesy lies in My name. I have not sent them, commanded them, nor spoken to them; they prophesy to you a false vision, divination, a worthless thing, and the deceit of their heart.'" Be careful what you read outside of the Bible. The way to test its Biblical truth is by the Bible. Seek God's face in all things. Allow the Holy Spirit to guide you. And don't buy into the "cultural" Jesus whom some use to push false doctrine and political agendas. Don't be naive. And don't be deceived. Have a great Lord's Day everyone.

"Beloved, do not believe every spirit, but test the spirits, whether they are of God; because many false prophets have gone out into the world." 1 John 4:1

Coffee and Prayers this Wednesday Morning.

The other day I was scrolling through some YouTube videos on my lunch break, looking for a specific video. I happened to come across one where some guy posted about a "perfect "holster for his pistol. After about 3 minutes, I turned it off. When he showed the holster, I knew it was garbage. But then when I heard him say "I got it at Walmart for $6", it was reinforced to me that it was garbage. This guy said "It's an air soft holster but will work great with any gun." Now in case you don't know, an "airsoft" pistol or rifle is a toy that shoots plastic BBs. This guy was touting carrying a real firearm in a holster meant for a toy.

Anyone who knows me knows that I'm a huge advocate of having a good quality holster for a firearm. If a holster has Velcro, is "one size fits all", or has a mag pouch attached to it, it's pretty much garbage. Now if you're simply going to keep your weapon on your nightstand and never carry it, well a cheap one is okay. But. If you're going to CARRY your pistol, a good quality holster is a must.

The guy in the video may think he's getting a "bargain" with a $6 holster. But I GUARANTEE YOU, if he carries his pistol in it, he will either at best have his pistol fall out of it at some point, or at worst, lose it completely, or worse still, an accidental discharge. It's sort of the same way with our spiritual lives. Yes, the easiest way is sometimes the "cheapest" when it comes to our spiritual lives. Some will say "I don't need to go to church; I can watch church on television." It's a "$6 holster" way of saying "I won't put forth any effort to go to church and worship with fellow believers." Meanwhile, there are people in other countries who walk for miles just to go to church and worship in a mud hut.

The country with the largest growth of Christian churches is China, believe it or not. And China is a country that can and will put you to death for your faith.

Some will give excuse after excuse for not attending. As long as the bills are paid, as long as the kids are fine and they are fine, church isn't relative. They don't stay at the altar giving thanks when God has answered their prayers.

They reserve Sunday as a "$6 holster", and sleep late , sit around, and think of a dozen excuses why church isn't "necessary."

"It's raining. It's too hot. It's too cold. It's too pretty to be inside. I need to rest. I've got too much to do." On and on.

Coffee and Prayers

Now some can't attend due to health reasons, work, and so on.

I'm talking about those who use the excuse "Well I can watch _____ on television..." Yes, there are many good televangelists. And there are about twice as many bad ones. And some very prominent who never preach the Gospel. Never preach the Cross, salvation, redemption. They never mention Jesus. It's only about how much you can have, and they can tell you how to get it for your gift of $_____.

As I said, there are good preachers on television also. But let me ask you this. When you're sick, or when your spouse or child is sick, can you text or call that preacher? Will he come to the hospital and pray with you and stay with you?

My pastor drove to Jackson and stayed with me until nearly midnight when Cindy was hospitalized. He wouldn't leave my side until he was assured that she was in a room and we had all that we needed.

If you find a television preacher to do that for you, please let everyone know.

Will his other viewers call you and check on you? Bring you food? Pick up your kid from school?

Coffee and Prayers

When you're all alone will anyone come kneel and pray with you?

My point is this. Yes church is full of hypocrites and sinners. I know because I can be both. But that's why I go to church. I need the presence of the Holy Spirit. I need my fellow believers. I need to hear the Word from my pastor. I need to see my wife lifting her hands in worship. I need to go to the altar and pray for others and have them pray for me.

I wouldn't trade my time in church for any amount of money. Don't let your time of worship be a $6 holster. It will fail you at some point. Give God your all and your best, your first and your best.

Have a great day everyone.

"Let us hold fast the confession of our hope without wavering, for He who promised is faithful. And let us consider one another in order to stir up love and good works, not forsaking the assembling of ourselves together, as is the manner of some, but exhorting one another, and so much the more as you see the Day approaching." Hebrews 10:23-25

Coffee and Prayers

Coffee and Prayers this Lord's Day.

During World War II, Signalman 3rd Class Elgin Staples was serving aboard the Cruiser USS Astoria as the ship supported the landings at Guadalcanal. Around 0200, the Astoria was hit by fire from a Japanese ship. One of the Astoria's gun turrets exploded, knocking Staples overboard. Staples was dazed and injured, but kept afloat by the inflatable life belt he had put on earlier. Staples and other survivors were rescued by the USS Bagley, and returned to the Astoria, as her Captain attempted to save the badly damaged ship by running her aground.

These attempts failed, the ship began to sink, and Staples, along with others, found himself again in the water. He was still wearing his life belt that had now saved his life for the second time.

Staples was returning home on leave when he pulled the life belt out that he still had. He began to look at this belt that had twice saved his life. He was amazed to see that it was manufactured by Firestone Tire and Rubber of Akron, Ohio. Staples hometown. He noticed a number stamped on it and was curious about what it was for. Upon returning home, he sat in his mother's kitchen, asking about all that had gone on while he'd been away. His mother told him that she had taken a job at Firestone to help the war effort.

Staples recounted the story of how he'd been blown overboard, and how twice the life belt had saved him. He jumped up and retrieved the life belt that had twice saved him to show his mother. "Mom, look! This belt saved my life, and it was made in your factory!" His mother looked at the belt, and noticed the number. She was barely able to whisper as she told him, "Son, that number. That's my number, my inspector's number. I inspected this belt!" The belt and this story, and a picture of Staples and his mother are on display in the National WWII Museum in New Orleans. At no time, in the heat of battle, did Elgin Staples stop and wonder about the life belt he was wearing. It was only after he was safe that he began to reflect about it. He perhaps wondered who in his hometown may have made it. He had no idea whatsoever that his own mother had inspected the inflatable belt that had worked PERFECTLY and saved his life not once, but twice.

How many of us ever think about what God has done for us just during the course of our everyday lives? Do we ever stop to think about the "life belts" God has made for us? Do we ever consider that few seconds delay in leaving somewhere just saved us from being in that car accident at the next intersection? There have been literally dozens of times when my life was spared by some seemingly "coincidental" occurrence. One time I recall is years ago when I was standing in the doorway of the squad room. An officer in the squad room was showing his new weapon. Another officer, down the hall, called my name to ask me something. I had taken three or four steps down the hall when a shot rang out. The officer in the squad room had accidentally discharged his weapon. The round ricocheted off the floor and went right through the doorway where I had been standing five seconds earlier. The round would have caught me right in the face.

Coincidence?

Not in my mind. God. I could recount dozens of times I narrowly escaped death bilaterally seconds, or just a few feet. There are likely many times we all do the same thing. There are also things that God spares us from that maybe aren't life threatening, but are from God to protect us from perhaps heartbreak, or some life changing event that isn't in His will for us. That job or position we really wanted but didn't get, and was eliminated just a couple of years later. That relationship that we wanted that God knew wasn't right for us. Everyone has their "life belt" story. Just as young Elgin

Coffee and Prayers

Staples had no idea that his own mother's work had saved his life, we often won't know how many times it is or was God's own hand that saves us. Have you considered that even those seemingly annoyances, hardships, and everything else in life could very well be God's life belt for you? Each day, take the time to reflect. Thank Him for His hand, His 'life belt" in your life.

You have been in the water, dazed and injured, so to speak. His "life belt" kept you afloat. Don't discount anything in life as "coincidence". Have a great day everyone. "I will lift up my eyes to the hills— From whence comes my help? My help comes from the Lord, Who made heaven and earth. He will not allow your foot to be moved; He who keeps you will not slumber. Behold, He who keeps Israel Shall neither slumber nor sleep. The Lord is your keeper; The Lord is your shade at your right hand. The sun shall not strike you by day, Nor the moon by night. The Lord shall preserve you from all evil; He shall preserve your soul. The Lord shall preserve your going out and your coming in From this time forth, and even forevermore." Psalm 121:1-8

Coffee and Prayers

Coffee and Prayers this Wednesday Morning.

I want to repost this that I wrote a while ago. I hope it helps at least one person today. The other day I watched the movie "Argo". It's based on the true incident in Tehran in 1979 when the embassy was taken over by Islamic militants. Six Americans were able to escape being held hostage as the others were, and were hiding in the Canadian embassy. The militants were going door to door seeking any Americans. The CIA called upon extraction expert Tony Mendez to come up with a plan to get the 6 out. After many options were considered, the only option viable to Mendez was to have the 6, along with himself, fly out commercially via Swiss Air. The plan was to have them pose as Canadian movie producers, script writers, and so on.

The cover story was that they were in Iran to scout locations for a sci-fi movie set in a desert like planet setting. The movie was titled "Argo". The 6 had to memorize "biographies" written just for them. There could be no mistakes if they were questioned at the many checkpoints. There was even a telephone number to the Los Angeles office on Mendez's business card .There would always be someone there to answer and verify the story. There was absolutely no other way to get them out. No other story was viable. They were in a hostile city of over a million people, most all of who wanted death to all Americans. The higher ups in the Carter administration thought the plan ridiculous.

The best quote was when Mendez said "There are no good options. There are only bad options. We have to use the best bad option." The six, along with Mendez, managed to get on a Swiss Air flight out of Iran and escape. The mission was classified for years. No one except those involved knew this was a CIA plan. It was just said that Canada helped the six Americans escape.

Life is like that at times. There we can be, just minding our own business in our own life and suddenly we are trapped in a situation not of our own making, or even due to our own mistakes. We have to do what we must do to get out alive and get back to normal. We may be surrounded all of a sudden by overwhelming odds. God will then sometimes provide us with a way that may not make sense to us. We have to get out but are fearful of the consequences we may face .Had the 6 Americans been caught in the embassy, they would be held as hostages. To be caught sneaking out using forged documents would mean immediate execution as spies. The risk of doing nothing, the greater risk of following God's plan until the end.

Coffee and Prayers

A huge decision.

The children of Israel had to immediately go into the midst of the Red Sea when God parted the waters. It seemed like a deadly choice despite the path that God opened for them. Some wanted to stay and just surrender to Pharaoh and go back to the life of slavery, the only life they'd ever known. We will face choices at times and there will sometimes be no "good" choices, only what seems at the time to be the "best bad option". God will have us at times to do what seems risky or even deadly, but when He has planned it, He will have all the pieces in place to bring it to pass. Have a great day everyone. "There are many plans in a man's heart, nevertheless the Lord's counsel- that will stand." Proverbs 19:21

Coffee and Prayers this Monday Morning.

Another work week begins. Yesterday I saw a video posted that was filmed in Destin. Some vacationers were filming a large hammerhead shark that was pursuing a fish. The people filming were in a high rise condo, on their balcony. They were trying to warn the swimmers, who couldn't see it. They eventually did see it and got out safely. The swimmers couldn't see it because they weren't looking from the same perspective. In the ocean, in water where you are up to your waist only, even in crystal clear water as that was, your view is limited. In water up to your neck, wearing a life jacket for example, you can only see a few feet around you, and only a small area above you. I've been out far in the ocean before. I know. It's an eerie feeling when you can literally not see the shoreline. Only my knowing which direction to swim until I could see the hi-rises onshore kept me from panicking. I couldn't see but a few feet around me, but I knew where to go.

Life is like this when we don't have faith in what God already has seen, already sees, already knows. We can't see but just a few feet around ourselves, but He sees it all.

He already knows the plans He has for us. Isaiah 46:10 says "Declaring the end from the beginning, And from ancient times things that are not yet done, Saying, 'My counsel shall stand, And I will do all My pleasure,'"

We flail and splash around cluelessly, oblivious to all when we have no faith in Him.

I, at my lowest points have just cried out to Him, declaring that I KNOW He didn't bring me that far

Coffee and Prayers

to leave me. I sometimes wonder humorously if He hadn't at times, wanted to put me in a headlock like Biff did to George McFly in "Back to the Future", rap His knuckles on my head and say "Hello?? Think Billy! THINK!" Would He ever just abandon me? No!

When we feel distant from Him it's because we've moved, not Him. We can see better what's all around us when we try to see from HIS perspective. We have to pray for the discernment to wisely go where HE leads us, and know He's there, and not just say, "Here's my plan Lord, come join me in it."

Are you so far out in the water, so deep in the water that you can't see what's around? Pray for faith and wisdom to try and see more from HIS perspective. Ask HIM which way to swim. When we understand His word, we gain abettor view of His plans, His thoughts towards us, and His love for us. We won't ever fully see with our limited view, but that's where, that's when a strong faith comes in.

He may do things or have us do things that make no sense at all. He's done that all through recorded time. Makes no sense to us, but we just need to trust Him.

Have a great day everyone.

Coffee and Prayers

"'For My thoughts are not your thoughts, nor are your ways My ways,' says the Lord.' For as the heavens are higher than the earth, So are My ways higher than your ways, And My thoughts than your thoughts.'" Isaiah 55:8-9

Coffee and Prayers this Freezing Cold Morning.

I posted this about a year ago. At the time I had a "friend" on here who wasn't a friend at all, and I knew it. This person only liked to look at my posts and go back to his friends, where he'd make fun of what I'd say. This person wanted to be an antagonist on everything I would write. I finally just decided to unfriend and give it no more ammunition.

I was thinking last night just before I went to sleep about how some people can be. How they can take something that we intended for good and try to turn it around and make it as if we are doing it out of evil intent, or for some "ulterior" motive. They judge our actions through the filters of their own egos or intents. No matter what you do, no matter what your heart in a matter, they will turn it around and try to use it against you.

Coffee and Prayers

When the king of Ammon died, David sent his servants to comfort Hanun, the king's son. Some of the people accused David of sending his servants there to spy out the land in an effort to conquer it. (2 Sam 10).

When the Ark was brought back to Jerusalem, David danced for joy in the streets. His wife Michal despised him for doing it. She thought it "undignified". She falsely accused him in what his intentions and heart was (2 Sam 6: 14-23).

Saul pursued David to try to kill him, and once when Saul went into a cave to relieve himself, David was so close to him in the dark that he cut off a piece of Saul's robe and later showed him that he had no intention of doing Saul harm . (1 Sam 24).

Our society has become so cynical that even the most devout Christians sometimes forget the words of Jesus, "Therefore, whatever you want men to do to you, do also to them, for this is the Law and the Prophets." Your translation may say "Do unto others as you would have them do unto you."

Years ago, small groups at Colonial Hills would do "Coke Events" (Conspiracy Of Kindness Events).

Coffee and Prayers

Some groups would give away ice cold canned drinks to drivers stopped at intersections on hot days. People would look upon this with suspicion. They'd try to "donate", and the purpose WASN'T to collect money. Some groups I seem to remember did free car washes, and people wanted to donate, or ask what was the catch. They couldn't believe there was anyone doing "something for nothing". In fact, money was flatly refused.

Someone posted the other day about how manners are so rare these days, when you show manners, you're accused of flirting.

People will draw their own conclusions on anything we do. Have you ever done something with the best intention, only to have someone think it was of some ulterior motive? This world has become more cynical. When you do something nice, people sometimes think "What is he/she up to?" Or they only know part of the situation and conclude the worse. All that we can do is the best that we can do. Seek God's will and seek His face. Pray for those who wrongly accuse us. Pray that He opens their eyes and opens their hearts. God may or may not work on them. All that we can do is to do what is right, what God leads us to do.

The important thing is that GOD knows our heart, our thoughts, our motivation. We have to be salt and light, hard as it is sometimes. And while we don't enjoy it when others misinterpret us, let's be careful to not jump to conclusions about others. Easy to say, hard to do.

Let's keep one another prayed up and lifted up.

Have a great day everyone.

"'Who am I, O Lord God? And what is my house, that You have brought me this far?'" 2 Sam 7:18

Coffee and Prayers this Again Hot Morning.

Stars visible from my front yard, but lighting back to the north. Most of the news the last week had been about the terrorist who killed 4 Marines and a Sailor in Chattanooga.

William Shakespeare wrote in "Julius Caesar" that "The good men do is interred with their bones, while the evil that they do lives on." In some ways, I don't disagree with that. Several days ago before this even happened I was thinking about how bad behavior is rewarded in our society. Especially when they are in a national spotlight. These people who are on the so-called "reality" shows gain more of an audience with their bad behavior. Celebrities gain more lucrative contracts and publicity the worse they behave.

Some in the elected office keep getting re-elected despite how badly they perform and how many scandals they get involved with. Then someone such as this man gets days upon days of non-stop mention of his name. Just what he wanted. He has the reward he wanted for the evil that he has committed. So where is God in all of this some are asking. Just as they did after 9/11. God is right where He was when His Son was being nailed to the cross. He is hurting over this more than any of the families are. God gives us free will. And evil, by the most basic logic, is the absence of good. Just as there is no such thing as 'cold.'

Cold is the absence of heat.

There is no such thing as darkness in itself, it is the absence of light. Evil is the absence of good, and God is the purest form of goodness and love. This man had an absence of God, therefore an absence of good. I grew up hearing that you should never question God. I have, however, in all these years learned that God is NOT afraid of honest questions. Questions asked out of honest inquiry and not anger or judgment because we are not in a position to judge God, nor question His MOTIVES. God is

Coffee and Prayers

NOT afraid of honest questions. I try to put things in perspective. How many of these tragedies and even worse does God stop? That we will never know. I know that He has by His divine mercy saved my life many times.

Yes, this is a tragedy.

A man plotted and planned to kill anyone around him. He planned this for months. His reasoning in it is beyond me. Just as the evil others commit, their reasoning is beyond comprehension, it's just pure evil. Every day we hear of children being killed by their own parents. Their own parents! We hear of it more and more. There are people being killed by terror attacks all across the globe. Then there are people who die of illness, car accidents, and so on. There are plane crashes that kill many more people than died in Chattanooga, and in Charleston a few weeks ago, yet we don't seem to question God as much for one or two lives as we do in a national tragedy. We don't seem to think they are as much of a tragedy.

To sum it all, I have to re-state what I said a week or so ago. I think about what God said to Job in Job 38 and 39.

Read those 2 chapters and put yourself in the place of Job. Imagine God asking you, "Where were you when I laid the foundation of the earth?" I chose to keep my trust in God. He allowed His Son, Jesus Christ to be crucified to pay for the sins of us all. Without my trust in, and acceptance of His being my Lord and Savior, then my sins would send me to hell just as fast as the sins of those who commit the most heinous crimes this nation, this world has ever seen. We see evil all around us. We see good people suffer while we see evil people flourish. It's frustrating but remember this. God will balance the books one day.

Have a great day everyone.

"Then the Lord answered Job out of the whirlwind and said: 'Who is this man who darkens counsel by words without knowledge? Now prepare yourself like a man; I will question you, and you shall answer Me. Where were you when I laid the foundations of the earth? Tell Me if you have an understanding.'" Job 38:1-4

Coffee and Prayers this Lord's Day.

With this part 3 of the little Noah series, I want to begin to look at how the flood of Noah, and the Ark is a symbol of our salvation.

Coffee and Prayers

Let's look outside of the ark. Noah and his sons spent 120 years building the ark to God's specifications. In the end, only 8 people in the entire world were safely inside it. But the doubt that kept all others out turned out to be deadly. Can you imagine what was said of Noah by those who lived around him? That crazy man who was ridiculed and laughed at? After all, he was building this huge vessel to supposedly float and there was no water around! He spoke of a disaster to come, a disaster of which they laughed at I would imagine. Scripture doesn't say so, but knowing human nature, and the fact that he built this thing and it took him 120 years. Only 8 people in the entire world didn't doubt.

In the movie "Noah", there rain was pouring inside the Ark. This would have never happened. Why? It's a symbol of our salvation. Our salvation has no "leaks". Also, God instructed Noah and his sons on the construction of the

Ark. Had it leaked, it would mean that God's plans were flawed.

Let's look at the diversity of those inside. There were 7 pairs of EVERY clean animal, and 2 of every UNCLEAN animal. Imagine the sight. Here were all of these animals. From small to large, birds of every kind, insects. All the different types and varieties and species. All together. A symbol of how all of us who are believers and are safe in Him, Jesus will be. Young and old, black and white and brown and yellow and everything in between that are in Him. Differing personalities, all secure.

The decision to be inside or not is sealed when the door is shut. Look at Gen 7:16. "And the Lord shut him in." God shut the door, Noah didn't. At that point, all were either sealed in or out.

The door that God shut is sealed from all outside forces, much as our salvation is. And no matter if the 8 who were on board were scared at times. It didn't matter what they "thought", their security was in what GOD DID. The doorways sealed, and our security in His salvation is sealed.

Once we are saved, we are sealed. There are some who believe that salvation can be lost. Jesus Himself said "No one is able to snatch them from My hand." Just as those 8 who were now sealed inside the ark.

This ark carried this massive load of animals and food and people and whatever else they needed. It had the strength to carry them. There was no danger of sinking, no danger of capsizing, no danger of the ark falling apart.

Coffee and Prayers

The security of those inside is sure. Storms and all else didn't matter. As they were carried safely in the ark, they couldn't steer, they couldn't sail, all they could do was to stay inside and trust God to take them safely to this brand-new world.

People doubted, and no doubt laughed at and scorned Noah. They wondered why he did what he did. All that mattered now was not what he did, but that God provided his salvation. And he and his family and the animals were saved.

We will be ridiculed by some. They will wonder why we do what we do. They will think us crazy for speaking of the coming judgement and urging others to repent and come inside. When the waters rise, we will have our security, those of us who are in Him.

Is your salvation assured? Are you in Him? Tomorrow we conclude this little series.

Have a great day everyone.

"They and every beast after its kind, all cattle after their kind, every creeping thing that creeps on the earth after its kind, and every bird after its kind, every bird of every sort. And they went into the ark to Noah, two by two, of all flesh in which is the breath of life. So those that entered, male and female of all flesh, went in as God had commanded him; and the Lord shut him in." Genesis 7:14-16

Coffee and Prayers this Wednesday Morning.

I see it often when I search some sites on Facebook, or search for videos on YouTube. There's always some site titled "20 Things You're Doing Wrong", or "Ten Things You're Doing Wrong", and so forth. Some things are called "life hacks", things to make life "easier."

It's usually something totally ridiculous that we are supposedly doing wrong, such as even getting into or getting out of a car.

I watch some just for entertainment, and I saw one the other day that said that we are all peeling bananas wrong, because monkeys peel bananas from the other end!

One said to store jeans in the freezer to remove the odors, enabling you to wear them many times before washing.

Coffee and Prayers

These are just a couple of many. Now personally, I don't feel that I need to look to the animal kingdom for tips on how to eat. Or anything else really. I'm not fond of how dogs greet each other and certainly wouldn't want to greet anyone that way.

And, as much as I hate doing laundry, I actually have more time to do laundry than I would have time to thaw out jeans. And storing dirty jeans where I store my ice and other frozen foods isn't a great idea to me either.

I got to thinking of this when a friend of mine posted a quote by Ronald Reagan about how congress would have changed up the Ten Commandments if it were up to them.

The world is like this with God's Word. The world tells us we are doing it wrong to live by His Word. They call the Ten Commandments "outdated". But can you imagine a world where everyone actually DID follow His Commandments? We could wipe out a vast majority of crime, disease, poverty, and so on.

Imagine if we all lived by Biblical principles? Imagine how we'd be treating people the way we want to be treated!

Coffee and Prayers

That alone would turn this world around. Imagine if all the pagan nations and people loved Jesus, and considered everyone their brother and sister? Imagine. God laid out His Word for us to follow.

He didn't lay it out as a "buffet", for us to just pick and choose what we like and leave the rest. Jesus said "He who is of God hears God's words; therefore you do not hear, because you are not of God." John 8:47

So we have websites that tell us how we are doing everyday tasks "wrong", we have the world telling us that the Judeo-Christian way of life is "wrong."

The world is telling us that the only thing that we should take from God's Word is these two words. "Judge not." And these two words are used out of context about 99% of the time.

We are to use all of God's Word.

"Jesus answered and said to them, 'Are you not therefore mistaken, because you do not know the Scriptures nor the power of God?'" Mark 12:24

God's Word works 100% of the time. It's more than a "hack" to make life easier. It shows the way to make our lives eternal through Jesus Christ.

Coffee and Prayers

There are tens of thousands of things that we are "doing wrong" in life. Things that lead to eternal damnation.

God tells us how to do all of life right. Have a great day everyone.

"Your word I have hidden in my heart, That I might not sin against You. Blessed are You, O Lord! Teach me Your statutes. With my lips I have declared All the judgments of Your mouth. I have rejoiced in the way of Your testimonies, As much as in all riches. I will meditate on Your precepts, And contemplate Your ways. I will delight myself in Your statutes; I will not forget Your word. Deal bountifully with Your servant, That I may live and keep Your word. Open my eyes, that I may see Wondrous things from Your law. I am a stranger in the earth; Do not hide Your commandments from me. My soul breaks with longing For Your judgments at all times. You rebuke the proud—the cursed, Who stray from Your commandments. Remove from me reproach and contempt, For I have kept Your testimonies. Princes also sit and speak against me, But Your servant meditates on Your statutes. Your testimonies also are my delight And my counselors." Psalm 119:11-24

Coffee and Prayers this Cold Thursday Morning.

I noticed a scene in the movie "The Dark Knight "the other day when I was flipping channels.

In one scene, Lucius Fox (Morgan Freeman), Bruce Wayne's business manager who funnels the equipment that Batman uses thorough Wayne Enterprises, was approached by an auditor who was going over the books at Wayne Enterprises. The auditor had realized that a super-secret military vehicle (not the campy convertible sedan that was previous the "Batmobile" in the old TV series) that Wayne Enterprises had built was the same one that was shown on the news in a chase a few nights before, and laid a set of blueprints on his desk. The auditor approached Lucius Fox and told him that he recognized the vehicle from blueprints he'd seen in his audits, and said that he wanted ten million dollars a year for the rest of his life to keep this secret.

Fox, smiling, then replies "So you think that your client, one of the richest and most powerful men in the world, is a vigilante who beats criminals to a pulp with his bare hands and your idea is to blackmail him.....Good luck."

Coffee and Prayers

The auditor then thinks about what he has just asked for and leaves the blueprints, realizing that he'd best keep his mouth shut.

It reminded me of how some lost people are when dealing with God's people. They will try anything. They try to harass, intimidate, steal from them, spread blatant lies about them, and even kill.

Jesus said this Himself "The thief does not come except to steal, and to kill, and to destroy. I have come that they may have life, and that they may have it more abundantly." John 10:10

But we serve a God Who is mightier than all. Their ideas on harming God's people is even a worse idea than a fictional character wanting to blackmail Batman.

There are many, many verses which speak of God's protection for His own.

Our God SPOKE this entire universe into existence. He placed the stars; He tells the oceans that they can go only so far. He numbers the clouds and the stars. He sees every living creature on the face of the earth, and in the deepest sea. He speaks life, He speaks healing, He raises the dead. He splits the sea for us to walk through. He placed the earth on nothing and set it the perfect distance from the sun

Coffee and Prayers

He created. He gives His angels authority and power, and only He knows their number. He gives us power through His Son Jesus Christ, Who died for our sins and they think it's a "good idea" to steal from us? To lie about us? To plan and plot all sorts of evil against us?

When we are His, we have His Word, His promises, His Holy Spirit and His Son Jesus. What can anyone do to us?

Have a great day everyone.

"He who dwells in the secret place of the Most High Shall abide under the shadow of the Almighty. I will say of the Lord, "He is my refuge and my fortress; My God, in Him I will trust." Surely He shall deliver you from the snare of the fowler And from the perilous pestilence. He shall cover you with His feathers, And under His wings you shall take refuge; His truth shall be your shield and buckler. You shall not be afraid of the terror by night, Nor of the arrow that flies by day, Nor of the pestilence that walks in darkness, Nor of the destruction that lays waste at noonday. A thousand may fall at your side, And ten thousand at your right hand; But it shall not come near you. Only with your eyes shall you look, And see the reward of the wicked. Because you have made the Lord, who is my refuge, Even the Most High, your

dwelling place, No evil shall befall you, Nor shall any plague come near your dwelling; For He shall give His angels charge over you, To keep you in all your ways. In their hands they shall bear you up, Lest you dash your foot against a stone. You shall tread upon the lion and the cobra, The young lion and the serpent you shall trample underfoot."
Psalm 91:1-13

Coffee and Prayers this Cloudy Saturday Morning.

The other day I was thinking about a movie I watched several years ago. The movie was "The Last of the Dogmen". It takes place in modern times in Montana. A bounty hunter, Lewis Gates, (Tom Berringer) tracks 3 escaped convicts into the Oxbow Quadrangle of Montana. As he comes across what looks like a slaughter, he discovers an arrow. He takes it to an archeologist named Lillian Sloan (Barbara Hershey). Sloan determines it's a Cheyenne arrow.

Gates researches and discovers that many people have "disappeared" in the oxbow. He and Sloan on horseback decide to venture into the oxbow and are captured by a band of Cheyenne who have been isolated from the world since the1860's. The Cheyenne here live as their tribe has for hundreds of years. It's only Sloan's ability to speak Cheyenne that saves them, as the Cheyenne speak only their language. As they are questioned by the Cheyenne at one point, the chief asks Sloan about the "silver birds with long tails." He's referring to planes and their contrails of course. Something the Cheyenne know nothing about.

Sloan tells them that there are people in those "birds" who can walk around and sit down. The Cheyenne all laugh, and call her a "wonderful liar." They think it's just a tall tale made up by Sloan.

It reminded me about how some people doubt or deny the existence of God because they've never experienced His answered prayers or had His blessings on their lives.

When we hear atheists talk about our "imaginary sky daddy" as they all say, we know that He's "imaginary" only in THEIR minds. He's as imaginary to some as that "silver bird" that carries people were to the Cheyenne in that movie. Of course Sloan had been ON one in her life. She had flown in one, sat in one, walked around in one. But to someone such as the Cheyenne, it was a lie.
Those of us who have known, have EXPERIENCED His answered prayers, experienced His healing,

experienced His hand in our lives and witnessed how He's done it in others' lives know Him to be real.

Some will want to try to treat God as a "Santa", or a genie, and they give Him a "shopping list", and they end up disappointed. It's then that they decide He's not real. God works in His own way. He works things out in His own timing. He's not a genie who grants 3 wishes.

Others disbelief doesn't change anything. Now there's no chance that Sloan could have convinced the Cheyenne what the truth about planes or any other modern day things truly are.

But did that change anything just because some didn't believe? Absolutely not.

How has God worked in your life? How has He NOT worked? Are you truly believing that He wants to best for you? Or are you frustrated at His seemingly not answering your prayers? Or do you not believe in Him at all?

(James 4:2-3 You lust and do not have. You murder and covet and cannot obtain. You fight and war. Yet you do not have because you do not ask. You ask and do not receive, because you ask amiss, that you may spend it on your pleasures.)

Coffee and Prayers

God only wants the best for His children. Don't let the unanswered prayers of unbelievers or others frustrate you. God works things out. It's easy for those who don't know Him to dismiss Him as a "lie". But those of us who have experienced Him know the truth. Have a great day everyone.

"For I know the thoughts that I think toward you, says the Lord, thoughts of peace and not of evil, to give you a future and a hope. Then you will call upon Me and go and pray to Me, and I will listen to you. And you will seek Me and find Me, when you search for Me with all your heart." Jeremiah 29:11-13

Coffee and Prayers this Thursday Morning.

The other day, I read where the Memphis Police Director now wants to get "input from the community" on how to handle police situations.

On the surface, some may think that this is a good idea. Let me ask you this.

Would you want "community input" deciding how your doctor handles your illnesses? How about if you're having surgery and your surgeon puts it on

Coffee and Prayers

Facebook live and then takes action based on the comments?

Would you want "community input" determining how your attorney handles your legal situation? What if you're in court and it's live on Facebook and your attorney decides to let the comments decide his or her actions in court?

So why would any acting Police Director want to rely on "community input" to determine policy?

If you ever read online news stories involving police and read the comments from the "community", you may wonder why most of THEM aren't locked up. And it's likely many of them have been.

Most likely, the "community" will always want to have the police ignore everything that they want to do that's illegal.

Most likely the "community" would render the police as nothing more than just another city entity. After all, most people feel as if the law shouldn't apply to themselves anyway.

So what about "community" doctrine, as far as faith issues? We see more and more that pastors and preachers are leaning more to ways to make people "feel good",

Coffee and Prayers

rather than teaching the Bible. Yes, we have to reach the lost where they are, no doubt, but telling them that their lifestyles that run contrary to the Bible are okay with God is not good. Jesus reached people WHERE THEY ARE, to bring them OUT of what they were IN.

We have a new movie playing in theaters now where God is completely misrepresented. Where Biblical truth is ignored, and instead a "feel good" message that basically seems to say that "I'm okay, you're okay, whatever you believe about God is okay , we are all saved and all are going to heaven. Don't worry about sin, repentance, judgement, and all that."

We have pastors and church leaders who like to tell people what they WANT to hear rather than what they NEED to hear. Yes the Bible is full of good news. It's full of redemption, forgiveness, joy, God sent His Son to meet us where we are and to SAVE US, not to just come here and throw a few platitudes at us about life and go on about His business. Jesus spoke of a coming judgment. He spoke of hell for the lost who refuse repentance. Anyone who says otherwise hasn't read their Bible.

Hosea 4:6 says "My people are destroyed for lack of knowledge..."

Coffee and Prayers

Yes I hate having my "toes stepped on" during a sermon, but you know what? My toes will get over it. If something in a sermon "hits home" with me then I know that the Holy Spirit is prodding me to work on that.

The Bible, His Word, who God, Jesus and the Holy Spirit is, is laid out CLEARLY in the Bible. When we as a society decide that we are going to change who they are and what they represent, then we are much worse than community policing, or doctoring, or being an attorney.

Don't let a movie or anyone steer you in a direction that is contrary to God's Word. Don't let anyone make you think that God is less than who He says He is and we KNOW is.

KNOW who He is through reading the Bible. Don't try to learn of Him through a movie or television show. Learn of who He truly is. Don't go along with the notion that it's okay to just keep Him in a bottle and just ignore Him until He's "needed." Don't go along with the crowd. The majority isn't always right.

Pray that He gives you wisdom and discernment. There are many deceiving spirits out there people.

Have a great day everyone.

Coffee and Prayers

"Then Jesus cried out and said, "He who believes in Me, believes not in Me but in Him who sent Me. And he who sees Me sees Him who sent Me. I have come as a light into the world, that whoever believes in Me should not abide in darkness. And if anyone hears My words and does not believe, I do not judge him; for I did not come to judge the world but to save the world. He who rejects Me, and does not receive My words, has that which judges him—the word that I have spoken will judge him in the last day. For I have not spoken on My own authority; but the Father who sent Me gave Me a command, what I should say and what I should speak. And I know that His command is everlasting life. Therefore, whatever I speak, just as the Father has told Me, so I speak." John 14:44-50

Coffee and Prayers this Cold Friday Morning.

Several years ago I went to see Chely Wright in concert. Although not world famous, she had several country hits in the late 90's and early 2000's.

I cannot remember exactly where the concert was, but it was a fairly small venue. Perhaps 1200 to 1500 people.

Coffee and Prayers

She was very personable, and did some interaction with the audience.

She asked various ones where they were from and so on. She asked who was from farthest away. One woman stood and said she was from Canada. She then said "Also, I know you! You and I have a connection through our mothers." "How so?" Chely asked her. "My mother bought your mother's house!" The woman mentioned the town in Ontario, but I cannot remember its name. "No, not MY mother's house." Chely replied. My mother lives in Kansas. She's lived there all her life. You must be thinking of Michelle Wright. She's from Canada, I'm from Kansas."

Michelle Wright is a country singer also, and is Canadian, and had several hits around the same time period.

The woman sat down, clearly embarrassed.

It was an honest mistake on the woman's part. No harm done except a little embarrassment for her. The two had the same last name, and similar first names.

Mistaken identity. It can result in something as harmless as a little embarrassment, to something as serious as eternal damnation.

Coffee and Prayers

This happens when people assume that they are following the ONE TRUE GOD, and they aren't.

They assume that all roads lead to salvation when they don't. They see some "feel good" movie where God is misrepresented, and they take the false doctrine of it to heart instead of following the Bible and knowing the TRUTH of His Word. One such movie is one that came out a while back called "The Shack." I'm not going to go into detail, but there is enough false doctrine and teaching in that movie to mislead a generation to hell. Yes, a few "feel good "lines, a few truths. But even one false thing about God makes it dangerous. Just as Clorox has water as a base ingredient, and water is harmless to drink, it's the other ingredients mixed with it that makes it poisonous. People also will think that because Buddha taught this or that, that it's okay to follow his teachings. Some follow Muhammad. And many people follow the teachings of L. Ron Hubbard, the founder of Scientology.

They mistakenly think also that a little Buddhism mixed with Christianity, or a little Islam mixed with Christianity, or a little Scientology mixed with Christianity is okay.

The thing is, when we die, we are going before Almighty God. We will have to stand before Jesus.

Coffee and Prayers

Buddha won't be there to judge. Neither will Mohamed or Hubbard. And unlike the woman at that concert, it won't be just a little embarrassing moment. It will have eternal consequences. Are you following the TRUE GOD of the Bible? Do you know Him? Do you have a personal relationship with Him? Or are you getting your "word" from Hollywood movies that just want to make you "feel good"?

The only way to be sure of His Word, His TRUE WORD, not the watered down, word and message of the world is to KNOW HIS WORD! To KNOW HIM! Eternal salvation rests upon it. Have a great day everyone.

"Not everyone who says to Me, 'Lord, Lord,' shall enter the kingdom of heaven, but he who does the will of My Father in heaven. Many will say to Me in that day, 'Lord, Lord, have we not prophesied in Your name, cast out demons in

Your name, and done many wonders in Your name?' And then I will declare to them, 'I never knew you; depart from Me, you who practice lawlessness!' "Therefore whoever hears these sayings of Mine, and does them, I will liken him to a wise man who built his house on the rock: and the rain descended, the floods came, and the winds blew and beat on that house; and it did not fall, for

it was founded on the rock. "But everyone who hears these sayings of Mine, and does not do them, will be like a foolish man who built his house on the sand: and the rain descended, the floods came, and the winds blew and beat on that house; and it fell. And great was its fall." And so it was, when Jesus had ended these sayings, that the people were astonished at His teaching, for He taught them as one having authority, and not as the scribes.
Matthew 7:21-29

Coffee and Prayers this Rainy Friday Morning.

The other day I was watching "Man of Steel", to me, a good incarnation of the Superman story. Superman has always been my favorite superhero since I was a kid. Since I used to read the comic books since I was a kid, I knew that the symbol on Superman's chest was not an "S", and didn't stand for "Superman". It is the symbol for the house of El, (his Kryptonian name is Kal-El, his father's name was Jor-El). In the movie, Lois Lane asks him "What does the S stand for?" He replies "It's not an S, it's my family symbol, it's the symbol of hope."

Many people, all their lives have thought that the S was for "Superman". Of course, it's only make believe, characters for comic books and movies. It's not that important in life is it? Not at all.

But what about what IS important to not have misconceptions about? The Bible is probably the most mid-quoted and misunderstood book in all of recorded history. There are so many misconceptions about what the Bible says. Even devout Christians sometimes misquote the Bible, take Bible verses out of context, and sometimes quote something they attribute to the Bible that is not even in the Bible at all.

Over the coming weeks, I would like to take a look at some of the "Bible myths", some of the most misquoted, most taken out of context, and non-Biblical sayings that are attributed to the Bible. A comic book icon or a movie character there are misconceptions about doesn't matter.

Misconceptions about the Bible DOES matter. This week alone I have heard 2 "leaders" from the largest denomination in the world speak blatant lies concerning the Bible. One said that Jesus was a "dreamer" (in reference to the USAs DACA program) Jesus was not brought to Egypt to be a citizen. Another said that hell was a concept "made up" by Christians. No, hell is a real place.

Coffee and Prayers

I would urge anyone who doesn't think so to read their Bible.

I think that one of the most misquoted verses in the Bible is "Money is the root of all evil." I've even heard some preachers say that "The Bible says money is the root of all evil." Well, is money the root of all evil?

What causes so many arguments in a marriage? Money arguments. The wife spends too much on whatever; the husband spends too much on whatever. One hides money from the other. One secretly loans or gives money to a friend or relatives. One wants to spend money on clothes or shoes. Money they don't have budgeted. One wants to spend money on his "hobby" they don't have budgeted. And then there is the other level. It causes arguments and marriage problems. Money is the root of it?

A drug habit that gets more and more expensive, personal money all spent, so theft sets in. Money at the root of it? Then there is just greed. Some just want more and more money. They need bigger and better "toys". They will do what it takes to make more money. They will stab a coworker in the back to get that promotion and the raise that goes with it.

Coffee and Prayers

We look at our city halls, our state capitols, and Washington DC. What gets so many in trouble? Money. Greed. Corruption. Money for favors. Money for favorable legislation.

Money the root of it all?

What about married couples? Suppose they love one another so much that they would NEVER, ever damage the family finances over a new wardrobe, a new car, a "hobby", or whatever. Suppose that when the wife needs or wants something, they sit down and discuss it out of love, and she doesn't sneak around and buy in secret? Suppose the husband wants or needs that new tool or whatever. Suppose he and his wife sits down to discuss it out of love? Wouldn't it be better than an argument when the bills are due and the checking account is way too low?

When someone wants a promotion at work, suppose he or she simply prays for it because they NEED the raise today bills, not to buy more. Would that person stab a coworker in the back for that promotion if they truly loved God?

Suppose those in power from city hall to DC loved God more than the power of the dollar? We would have a lot of less wealthy people in power, and our nation would prosper.

Coffee and Prayers

So IS money the root of all evil? Well we ALL have bills to pay. None of us are bill free. We incur mortgage debt , we have to have a vehicle , we have to pay light, gas, water and phone bills unless we chose to become as the Amish in that aspect . We have to have money these days. We have taxes to pay and have no choice in that. Even Jesus, in Matt 17:27 told His disciples to cast out their line, and in the first fish's mouth they would find a coin to use to pay the tax.

So, what verse says "Money is the root of all evil"? It doesn't. 1 Tim 6:10 is misquoted.

It says the LOVE of money is a root of all kinds of evil. It's not money itself, but the LOVE of money. The love of money more than the love of spouse. The love of money more than the love of children. The love of money more than the love of family, the love of fellow man. The love of money more than the love of those who elected officials are supposed to SERVE.

It's not money in itself, it's when the love of that money takes first place. I've seen families split up over love of money. A family member thinks that he or she is entitled to have that which another has. Love of money causes jealously, envy, strife, hatred.

Coffee and Prayers

We've seen hundreds and hundreds of people arrested and jailed because at some point, money was desired overall else.

If we love our spouse over money, love our family over money, love our fellow man over money, love our Savior over money, there won't ever be a time that we have to stand before our God and be guilty of trading the love of money over a human being. It's not money that is evil, but the love of it. Where is your love? Have a great day everyone.

"For the love of money is a root of all kinds of evil, for which some have strayed from the faith in their greediness, and pierced themselves through with many sorrows." 1 Timothy 6:10

Coffee and Prayers, My Usual Routine.

The morning air is hot, heavy, and still even long before sunrise.

I was thinking this morning about another story that my Grandmother Ellis told me that happened in the early '80s. Late one stormy night she got a call from her brother Earl who lived on his farm, alone down in Morgan City, MS, and suffered from emphysema. He said, "Sis, please come help me, I'm so sick." She had been windowed since '71 and had no one around to go with her. There were tornado warnings all through that night. Severe thunderstorms and all that occurs with them. High winds and torrential rain.

As she got her things together and got in her car to make the drive in such conditions she said that she prayed, "Lord, please help me make it to his house safely." Her drive consisted mostly of back roads, from Harmony Road

in Carroll County, down to the other side of Morgan City. Tress limbs were blowing down everywhere. The rain on the dark roads made it hard to see. But she said that she felt a hand, a real hand on her shoulder that night. As if someone were in the backseat and had a hand on her shoulder.

That touch took the fear out of her and she never had any doubt that she would make the trip safely. She made it safely and took care of her brother that night, and for the next couple of days. She never forgot about that feeling of how the Lord literally had His hand on her shoulder that night and guided her through the storms. How many times do we experience that? Either in a literal storm or just in the "storms" of life? When we pray for His protection and seek His face in all that we do, He is faithful and just as Jehova Jireh, the Lord Who provides, Jehova Rapha, the Lord Who heals, Jehova Nissi, the Lord our Protector (Banner), Jehova Shalom, the Lord our Peace. No matter how many stormy nights or miles of danger we face, He is there.

Never sleeping, never slumbering.

Always there.

Have a great Thursday everyone.

"Be merciful to me, O God, be merciful to me! For my soul trusts in You; And in the shadow of Your wings I will make my refuge until these calamities have passed by. I will cry out to God Most High, to God who performs all things for me. He shall send from heaven and save me.' Psalm 57:1-3

Coffee and Prayers. It's Thursday and the Weekend is in Sight.

Several years ago I heard a story about a missionary who lived in Bolivia. One day a woman was running and screaming for help. An enormous 20 foot long, 300 pound python was in her little house. The missionary grabbed a rifle, and through the window, took aim and hit the snake in the head with one well-placed shot. The giant snake began its death throes and in the process, nearly destroyed the little house as it thrashed around. The snake, for all practical purposes, was dead. Its system just didn't know it yet, and it did tremendous damage.

That is, in a way, how it is with Satan. Jesus crushed his head on the cross. Satan's death throes and thrashing about is causing a lot more damage. In his last ditch effort, he is killing unborn babies and trying to convince as many as he can that it's ok to do so. He's telling as many people as he can that God's word is a lie, or at best irrelevant. He's convincing as many as he can that they should never compare a person's actions to what God's word says. He's convincing people that we should not use God's word as a tool for discernment as to what sin is. He's convincing people that it is them and them alone who should decide what is right, not some old Book written so long ago.

Satan, as has always been the case since the beginning of time, twists God's word as he did with Eve. "Has God said…" Satan asked Eve. And when Eve told the devil that God said, he called her a liar. Adam and Eve both believed the lie instead of God.

Coffee and Prayers

And it cost them.

We have many people today who don't believe what God said.

I've heard "Judge not" and "Who are we to judge" so much the last few years and especially the last few days.

That verse is the most misquoted and misunderstood in the Bible.

I've even had one person say that we are to accept other's sin or else we are judging and therefore sinning! Nowhere. I mean NOWHERE in the Bible does it say that we must accept sin.

Yes Jesus loves us, and that's why He died, to pay for our sins. That's why He commands us to "Go and sin no more." He never says to continue on in them. Christianity and Judaism is vilified while Islam is elevated. It's more damage by the thrashing of a dead serpent.

I read only yesterday that not only is there a rise in those who approve of abortion, there are many who believe that a child up to age six should be killed by parents if they don't want the child!

It's sickening to see what is going on around us.

Coffee and Prayers

I truly don't know it it's the end, the beginning of the end, or the end of the beginning.

What I do know is this. The future has already been determined. There are no "alternative endings." God has won, so we have won. As I've said before, any day now our Father may say "Son, go and get My children."

Are you ready to go meet Him when He steps out on a cloud to call us? I sure hope so. I want to see you all there.

Have a great day everyone.

"Now I saw a new heaven and a new earth, for the first heaven and the first earth had passed away. Also there was no more sea. Then I, John, saw the holy city, New Jerusalem, coming down out of heaven from God, prepared as a bride adorned for her husband. And I heard a loud voice from heaven saying, "Behold, the tabernacle of God *is* with men, and He will dwell with them, and they shall be His people. God Himself will be with them *and be* their God. And God will wipe away every tear from their eyes; there shall be no more death, nor sorrow, nor crying. There shall be no more pain, for the former things have passed away."

Then He who sat on the throne said, "Behold, I make all things new." And He said to me, "Write, for these words are true and faithful."

And He said to me, "It is done! I am the Alpha and the Omega, the Beginning and the End. I will give of the fountain of the water of life freely to him who thirsts. He who overcomes shall inherit all things, and I will be his God and he shall be My son. But the cowardly, unbelieving, abominable, murderers, sexually immoral, sorcerers, idolaters, and all liars shall have their part in the lake which burns with fire and brimstone, which is the second death."
Revelation 21:1-8

Coffee and Prayers this Cold Friday Morning.

Glad that most of the 7 inches of "global warming" is gone.

I was thinking about "close calls" the other day as I made a joke about my "missing" the Oscars on TV made me feel like the guy on "Titanic" who had lost his ticket in a poker game just minutes before she sailed. It got me to thinking about maybe how many people perhaps wanted to take Titanic to America that day and for some reason couldn't.

Weren't they glad that they didn't? Weren't they thankful that they missed the trip for whatever reason after the heard of her sinking?

I remember after the terror attacks on 9-11, I heard of friends who were supposed to be in an office in the Pentagon. For one reason or another they were not on site that day, or were on the other side of the building. The plane hit where they were SUPPOSED to have been that day.

When I worked for the police department, I was standing in the doorway to the squad room at the station one day. An officer in the squad room was admiring his new Sig. Another officer called me, I left where I was standing to go see what he wanted, ten seconds later "BANG"! The officer's weapon went off, the bullet hit the floor and ricocheted through the door where I had just been standing seconds earlier! Had I still been there, I would have been hit.

I have been sitting at a red light, been distracted by the radio or something else, then when it turned green had someone blow through the light, missing me by just a few seconds because I had not immediately went when the light turned green.

Coffee and Prayers

Have you ever spent just a few minutes distracted by something, maybe looking for something, was just a few minutes late in leaving and then got down the street only to find a bad accident had just happened? Perhaps an accident that you would have been involved in had you left just minutes earlier?

There are perhaps many times each week that God protects us from some hidden danger or harm and we never even realize it.

Perhaps it's something to think about. When our day is hectic, when we are distracted by many things, God is alert to our needs. He is always there. That doesn't mean that we will never face danger, harm, or be in a life or death situation.

Just think about how many times a day we miss harm or danger because His hand is on us.

Have a great day everyone.

"Though I walk in the midst of trouble, You will revive me; You will stretch out Your hand against the wrath of my enemies, and Your right hand will save me." Psalm 138:7

Coffee and Prayers

Coffee and Prayers this Cool Tuesday Morning.

I'm glad to be back on my main Facebook profile.

Several years ago, me and one of my daughters were driving somewhere, and we both needed a restroom break. The women's room was either out of order or occupied, so I checked the men's room which was empty, and she used it while I stood guard. As she washed and dried her hands, she noticed the "cologne" dispenser next to the hand dryer.

"So THATS where that comes from!" She exclaimed. "What are you talking about?" I asked her. "In that song!" She replied, "Before he cheats. That Carrie Underwood song! The words 'right now, he's prob'ly dabbing on $3 worth of that bathroom Polo'"! She went on to explain. "I never had any idea what that meant until now."

"Yeah, these cologne dispensers are in a lot of restrooms. Not that I'd ever use any kind of so called cologne sold from a men's room." I told her.

I know this is a strange segway to my point, but sometimes the Holy Spirit will just reveal something in much the same way.

Coffee and Prayers

We can sometimes read or hear a verse and not really think much about it, and then the Spirit will just reveal it to us.

We may hear it in church and the pastor will reveal it in a way we've never thought of. We may hear it on the radio or television, and the Spirit will reveal a meaning that we've never thought about.

I've had many things revealed to me like that. It was that way for me with Genesis 7:16 "So those that entered, male and female of all flesh, went in as God had commanded him; and the Lord shut him in." I had read it many times, but it was when the Holy Spirit revealed to me that "shut him in" was symbolic of our salvation.

It's when we are in constant prayer and truly seeking in His Word that the Spirit will make the "Logos" (written word) become the "Rhema", the LIVING WORD.

Always be open to the ways that He will reveal His Word to you. Stay in prayer that you keep your heart, mind and spirit open to what He will reveal to you.

You never know where and when He will suddenly reveal that answer or answers you've been seeking.

Have a great day everyone.

"But God has revealed them to us through His Spirit. For the Spirit searches all things, yes, the deep things of God. For what man knows the things of a man except the spirit of the man which is in him? Even so no one knows the things of God except the Spirit of God. Now we have received, not the spirit of the world, but the Spirit who is from God, that we might know the things that have been freely given to us by God." 1 Corinthians 2:10-12

Coffee and Prayers this Rainy Monday Morning.

A lot of lightning and thunder last night, but sunshine forecast for today. I was thinking last night about a movie that I have always enjoyed. The movie is "City Slickers". It is a comedy with some dramatic moments about 3 life-long friends from New York City, Mitch, Phil, and Ed.

Coffee and Prayers

It's sort of a "coming of age" type movie for 30 something's. The main character, Mitch, has just turned 39. He has a great wife, a teen daughter, and a young son. Mitch sells commercial air time on a local NYC radio station. Phil has wife and kids, and runs a grocery store for his father in law. His wife is a mean woman, and very unpleasant to everyone. Ed runs a sporting goods store and has just married a 24 year old model. All three grew up together and have been friends since they were kids. Mitch, as I said, just turned 39 and is going through a "mid-life crisis". He hates his job and is making his family miserable.

Phil and Ed decide to surprise him on his birthday with a gift of a cattle drive. A 2-week horseback adventure working on a ranch in New Mexico, driving cattle on horseback to a ranch in Colorado. There are of course ranch hands and some other "guests" who pay to do this for 2 weeks, sleeping under the stars, riding and roping. As they go along a day or two into the drive they begin discussing their "best day, and worst day". They aren't allowed to say "the day their kids are born", as it is too easy. Mitch describes how his best day was when he was a kid and his dad took him to see his first Yankees game. He had never seen Yankee stadium except on a black and white TV.

Coffee and Prayers

His worst day was when his wife Barbara had a cancer scare, and the entire day waiting on test results was his worst. Phil, surprisingly, said that his best day was his wedding day. He said that just before the vows, his dad gave him a wink and he knew that he was a man then, and no longer a kid. When asked what his worst day was, they all laughed when he said "every day since then has been a tie." Ed decided at first that he didn't want to participate. The he decided that he would. As they rode their horses, he described how he was 15, and his abusive father came home one day and had his girlfriend in the car with him. He had always been abusive to Ed's mom, and to him and his sister.

Ed said that he finally that day stood up to him. He told his father that they didn't want him around any longer. He told him that he would take care of his sister and his mother. His dad drew back as if he was going to hit him, and Ed didn't flinch. He stood his ground. His father left and they never saw him again. He said that was his best day, standing up to his abusive father. When asked what his worst day was he replied "The same day." We all can relate to the "best day-worst day" scenario. We can all look back with a smile or with a heavy heart upon these days. It is our response to both that helps define who we are.

Coffee and Prayers

On our best days are we grateful to God? On our worst are we leaning on Him for strength?

I can think back on several of these. I know there have been several days that without the strength of the Lord I surely would have just died. We have family and friends that we lean on, the ones who God has placed into our lives. He uses them to comfort us as well. In our best days we should praise Him. In our worst days, we should lean on Him AND still praise Him. It can be hard to praise him in the storms of our life. But He is still God in the storms, our worst days. He is God in the sunshine, our best days. There are days when I remind myself what He has told me "I will never leave you nor forsake you." No matter what my day is or my days are. No matter, He is still there. Have a great day my friends. "For I, the LORD your God, will hold your right hand, Saying to you, 'Fear not, I will help you.'" Isaiah 41:13

Coffee and Prayers

In Remembrance

I will never forget the phone call I received on October 4th, 2018. It still seems like it was yesterday. Billy was having a massive heart attack and told Cindy to "call Pastor." We were on the road returning from visiting family in Michigan and had pulled over in Blytheville, Arkansas to get gas. I immediately pleaded with the Lord to spare Billy's life, however God decided to take him home. I wasn't ready to let him go. He was not only my member, but he had become one of my closest friends.

There are three things I will always remember about Billy: His smile, his love for others, and his love for his country. Life will never be the same without him, but Heaven is sweeter because he is there. I miss you Billy, but God's word assures me that I will see you again!

- Pastor James McElroy

Coffee and Prayers

www.ingramcontent.com/pod-product-compliance
Lightning Source LLC
Chambersburg PA
CBHW050312120526
44592CB00014B/1872